HUMAN RIGHTS
AND THE
INTERNATIONAL
COMMUNITY

For more than fifteen years, Egon Schwelb was Deputy Director of the United Nations Division of Human Rights. He also was the Secretary of the Main Committee of the United Nations General Assembly which has jurisdiction in social, humanitarian and cultural matters, the Third Committee.

On retiring from the United Nations Secretariat in the fall of 1962, he was appointed to the faculty of the Yale Law School, where he is engaged in research, writing, and teaching about those branches of International Law and of the Law of International Organization which are concerned with the protection of human rights.

Before joining the United Nations in 1947, he was the Senior Legal Officer of the United Nations War Crimes Commission in London.

He holds law degrees from the Universities of Prague and London.

Before the Second World War he practiced law in his native Prague and held various offices in the public life of Czechoslovakia. When Hitler invaded Czechoslovakia in 1939, Dr. Schwelb was imprisoned by the Gestapo, but he escaped to England just a few days before the outbreak of the war. During the war he served as a member of the Legal Council of the Czechoslovak Government-in-Exile in London.

Throughout his career, as a young lawyer in Czechoslovakia and, later, on the international scene, he has published widely on questions of constitutional and administrative law and Public International Law.

Freedom of the Press (1933), the Judicial Control of the Administration (1937), the Status of Foreign Forces (e.g., the status of American Forces in Britain during the War) (1944), Crimes against Humanity (1946), the Amending Procedure of Constitutions of International Organizations (1954), and various topical human rights problems have been among the subjects of the many studies which he has published.

HUMAN RIGHTS AND THE INTERNATIONAL COMMUNITY

The Roots and Growth of the
Universal Declaration of Human Rights, 1948-1963

by EGON SCHWELB

Published for the
B'nai B'rith, International Council,
Anti-Defamation League of B'nai B'rith,
and the United States Committee for the United Nations
by
QUADRANGLE BOOKS / *Chicago*

CONTENTS

INTRODUCTION

The late John Fitzgerald Kennedy, in his memorable speech at American University (June 10, 1963), underscored what human rights means in our world today. The very security of peace and freedom, President Kennedy clearly demonstrated, rests on a universal respect for and observance of these rights. The experiences of this generation echo his words: history must forever live with the profound tragedy of a world plunged into a devastating holocaust by an ideology born of contempt for man and his God-given dignity.

Fifteen years ago, on December 10, 1948, the United Nations General Assembly unanimously adopted the Universal Declaration of Human Rights. It did so because "the inherent dignity and ... the equal and inalienable rights of all members of the human family is the foundation of ... peace in the world." This historic document—a "Magna Carta of Mankind," in the phrase of U Thant —is the standard for men and nations who strive to promote the purposes and aims of the United Nations Charter.

B'nai B'rith, with its traditional concern for human rights, and in response to the invitation of the United Nations welcoming commemorative activities by non-governmental organizations on the Fifteenth Anniversary of the Declaration is pleased to be associated with the publication of this study by Dr. Egon Schwelb of the Yale University Law School. Dr. Schwelb, who formerly served as Deputy Director of the UN Division of Human Rights probes the roots of the Declaration, systematically analyzing its development from 1948 until the present. In the process, he strengthens our knowledge of the inspirations and motivations for the Declaration. We believe this study will be a valuable resource for those who concern themselves with assessing the meaning, significance and impact of the Universal Declaration of Human Rights.

Perhaps the most significant aspect of Dr. Schwelb's work is his thesis that the Universal Declaration, in the course of its history, has taken on the character of something more than a moral manifesto. It offers an encouraging response to those who are impatient with a continuing delay in the formulation and adoption of legal covenants on human rights. Dr. Schwelb shows us that the distinction between such international covenants and the Universal Declaration is becoming, through time and practice, increasingly blurred, and the Declaration itself, in the nobility of its purpose, is acquiring the force of law.

The progress that has been made in translating the Declaration into norms of international conscience and conduct should be an encouraging prod to every civilized nation in its responsibility to erase racial and religious discrimination, to combat human oppression, to denounce and overcome the kind of inhuman bigotry that explodes in the violence of a bombing or a shooting. All of these persist, too painfully, in our midst.

The United Nations Charter proclaims man's need "to practice tolerance and live together in peace." In this age of the missile and the hydrogen bomb, there is no real alternative. We are dependent on each other—and on man's inherent belief in justice and on his infinite capacity for goodness.

December 10, 1963   LABEL A. KATZ
                                 President of B'nai B'rith

This study is intended as a contribution to the world-wide commemoration of the fifteenth anniversary of the adoption, on December 10, 1948, of the Universal Declaration of Human Rights. It has been my ambition to make it a worthy companion volume to *A Living Bill of Rights* by Justice William O. Douglas, published in this series of *The One Nation Library*, which its distinguished author dedicated "To our high school students from Alaska to Puerto Rico, from Maine to Hawaii."

The American Bill of Rights has been in force for over 170 years. It has affected and continues to affect the life of every American. Its application by the Supreme Court and the respect or disrespect shown it by other authorities is one of the central themes of American history and of current events in the United States.

The Universal Declaration of Human Rights of December 10, 1948, on the other hand, has not, or not yet, played a comparable role in the reader's experience. It is part of a movement which is still in its beginnings. Subject to important exceptions, which will be described in this volume, it has not yet penetrated into the daily life of the peoples of the world.

In 1958, Mr. Dag Hammarskjold, the late Secretary-General of the United Nations, stated that the Declaration has acquired an authority of growing importance and that it was—he used the same term as Justice Douglas—a *living* document. In the pages that follow, an attempt will be made to prove not only that Mr. Hammarskjold was right in 1958, but that in the five years which have passed since, the Declaration has proved to be a more dynamic instrument than was believed when its Tenth Anniversary was being commemorated. The Declaration was proclaimed by the General Assembly as the first part of the "International Bill of Human Rights" with one or more "Covenants on Human Rights" and the "measures of implementation" soon to follow. The Covenants have not yet been adopted and the completion of the International Bill of Rights has been delayed for more than fifteen years. The Declaration, which for such a long period has been the only existing part of the International Bill of Rights, has assumed a far greater measure of importance than many of its authors intended. In the fifteen years since 1948, the political face of the world has undergone fundamental changes which brought in their wake a transformation of the constitutional set-up of the United Nations. In this changed and changing world the Declaration of 1948 has filled a vacuum.

The history of drafting the Declaration has often been described; its individual provisions have been repeatedly commented upon. The reader will find references to these very useful works of literature in Appendix I. In order not to repeat what has been so well done elsewhere, I have concentrated in the first part of this volume on the historical roots of the human rights provisions of the Charter and of the Universal Declaration of Human Rights and, in its second part, on the developments in the years since 1948, the period in which the surprising and unprecedented growth of the Declaration into an instrument of very great authority has occurred.

Appendix II contains the text of the most important documents with which the volume deals, and Appendix III is a list of other international instruments in the human rights field which it has not been possible to reproduce.

The manuscript of this volume was completed in July, 1963. For technical reasons beyond the publishers' and the writer's control, the printing was delayed. This fact has made it possible to insert in the text and in Appendix II references to important developments which took place in the course of the eighteenth session of the General Assembly (September to December, 1963).

The Yale Law School
New Haven, Connecticut
December, 1963

EGON SCHWELB

PART ONE

The Roots

A PARADOX: AN ORGANIZATION OF GOVERNMENTS CALLED UPON TO GIVE PROTECTION AGAINST GOVERNMENTS

The United Nations is an organization of governments. One of its principal purposes is the promotion and encouragement of respect for human rights and for fundamental freedoms for all without distinction as to race, sex, language, or religion.

The question of human rights is mostly, though not always, a question of the relationship between the individual and the government of his State; and it is the State against which the human rights of the individual are in need of protection. We are faced, therefore, with an organization of States, an organization of governments, which has been charged with the task of assisting in the realization of human rights vis-a-vis the States and governments themselves. This is an apparent or, in the view of some, a real paradox which has made the human rights activities of the United Nations a very delicate and difficult operation.

We will therefore address ourselves first to the question of how it came about that there is in existence an organization of originally fifty-one and now 113 governments expected to engage in the task of protecting their own citizens against themselves.

To explain the paradox it is necessary to recall some historical facts and developments.

The great American legal scholar, Roscoe Pound, once said (in 1928):

"Something was never made from nothing. Institutions do not spring Minerva-like full fledged from the heads of rulers or statesmen or lawmakers. Hence it need not surprise us when we are told that Magna Carta, which we put as the beginning of constitutional law, had yet its forerunners. It goes back, so we are now taught, by way of the charter of liberties of Henry the Second and the like charters of Stephen and Henry the First, to the charter of liberties of Cnut. This, however, is only its formal pedigree. In substance it is another thing. In substance it formulates ideas and realizes principles which are at the foundation of medieval social and political life."

The Universal Declaration of Human Rights of 1948 did not spring ready-made from the heads of a group of men and women (I should rather say: women and men, as they were mostly presided over by Mrs. Eleanor Roosevelt) who met in 1946, 1947, and 1948 at New York, Lake Success, Geneva, and Paris. In the following pages we shall investigate the Declaration's philosophical and constitutional roots and foundations and, to this end, enter upon a short analysis of the history, national and international, which led up to the adoption of the Declaration in 1948.

THE HISTORICAL FOUNDATIONS
OF THE DECLARATION

The Declaration's roots are in the legal and political thought of the seventeenth to the twentieth centuries: in the England of the *seventeenth century*, where "the immemorial rights of Englishmen" were developed, with the landmarks of the English Petition of Rights (1627), the Habeas Corpus Act (1679), the English Bill of Rights (1688) and the Act of Settlement (1700); a system of rights which was taken by colonists to the new world, where they were further developed.

In the *eighteenth century*, the era of rational humanism which sought to secure the basic rights for all men, the landmarks in this country were the Declaration of Independence; the Virginia Bill of Rights (1776) and similar achievements in other American colonies; the Constitution (1789) and the Bill of Rights, i.e., the first ten Amendments to the Constitution (1791) and the post-Civil War Amendments. In Europe the decisive event of the eighteenth century was the French Revolution and in its wake the Declaration of the Rights of Man and of the Citizen (1789) of which the English historian, Lord Acton, has said that its single confused page outweighs libraries and was stronger than all the armies of Napoleon. The French Declaration of the Rights of Man and of the Citizen was greatly influenced by the American Bills of Rights which, in their turn, reflected the French philosophy of the eighteenth century.

In the course of the *nineteenth and twentieth centuries*, the example set by the United States and France of adopting Bills of Rights or otherwise embodying such rights in their constitutions was followed in the entire Continent of Europe, West and East, and the movement spread to the Americas, Asia, and, recently, Africa. The democratic labor movement as well as the influence of the Russian revolution of 1917 added the ideas of economic equality and social and cultural rights to the heritage bequeathed by the English, American, and French revolutions. The first constitutional instruments in which these ideas found systematic expression were the Weimar Constitution of Germany (1919) and the Republican Constitution of Spain (1931).

INTERNATIONAL ACTION

Attempts to seek a foundation for the inalienable rights of the individual in the law of nations go back to an early stage in the history of international law. The greatest figures in the literature of international law in the seventeenth and eighteenth centuries, including, to some extent, Hugo Grotius, the "Father of the Law of Nations" [his work *De Jure Belli ac Pacis* appeared in 1625] exercised a powerful influence on the growth and acceptance of the concept of the inalienable rights of man. It has been said "that the law of nations, in itself conceivable only as being above the legal order of sovereign States, is not only a law governing their mutual relations but is also, upon final analysis, the universal law of humanity in which the individual human being as the ultimate unit of all law rises sovereign over the limited province of the State" (Lauterpacht, 120).

There have been two distinct channels and lines of action through which attempts were made to improve the lot of the citizens and inhabitants, first of particular States and, later, of all States, by international action: the so-called "humanitarian intervention" and the adoption of international treaties, conventions and declarations.

HUMANITARIAN INTERVENTION

Because of the danger of abuse inherent in "humanitarian intervention," the doctrine underlying it has never become a fully acknowledged part of international law; such action has rarely been effective, but it paved the way for the provisions relating to human rights of the Charter of the United Nations of 1945. In traditional international law it was assumed that a sovereign State had the authority to treat its own nationals according to its own discretion. When, however, the treatment meted out by a State to its own population, particularly to minorities, was so arbitrary, persistently abusive, and cruel that it shocked the conscience of mankind, other States, usually the great powers of the period, took it upon themselves to threaten, or even to use, force in order to come to the rescue of the oppressed minority. An early example of such "humanitarian intervention" was the action, including military action, agreed upon in 1827 by Great Britain, France, and Russia against the Ottoman Empire to bring to an end the sufferings of the Greek population then under Turkish rule. This intervention eventually led to the independence of Greece in 1830. Similar interventions were undertaken by several European Powers to put an end to the massacres of Christians in Syria (1860), to bring relief to the persecuted Christian population in Crete (1866-1868), to end Turkish misrule and persecutions of the Christian populations in Bosnia, Herzegovina (now parts of Yugoslavia), Bulgaria (1877-1878), and Macedonia 1903-1908). Other examples of humanitarian intervention were successive representations or protests made by Austria, France, Great Britain, and the United States on behalf of the Jewish population of Romania which had been the victim of persecution and attempts at extermination (1867-1902), and successive representations or protests made by the United States to the Russian Government on behalf of the persecuted Jewish citizens of Russia. The representations made to the Belgian Government concerning the atrocities in the Congo in 1906-1907, although in part based on a treaty commitment, also belong in this category. In the case of the persecution and eventual murder of millions of Jews by the Nazi regime in the thirties and forties of this century, such action as was taken by the powers of Europe and America while there was still time to help, did not go beyond ineffectual protests; after World War II, the punishment of some of the responsible criminals followed.

Protection of religious minorities

The method of concluding international treaties for the protection of religious minorities can be traced back to the seventeenth century. The Treaty of Westphalia (1648), which concluded the Thirty Years War, established for Germany the principle that there should be equality of rights for both the Roman Catholic and Protestant religions. In the same century various Catholic Governments stipulated in peace treaties for the rights of Roman Catholic subjects of Protestant Princes. In 1774, Turkey undertook vis-a-vis Russia to protect the Christian religion and its churches.

The Congress of Vienna and the Status of the Jews

The Congress of Vienna of 1815 provided for the free exercise of religion, and for equality, irrespective of religion, in various cantons of Switzerland and for the equality of the Christian religions in Germany. The Congress of Vienna also agreed on what probably is the first provision included in an international treaty and instrument aiming at the improvement of the status of Jews. The Constitution of the German Confederation on which the Sovereign Princes and Free Cities of Germany agreed on June 8, 1815, as well as the Act of the Congress on which all Powers represented at Vienna agreed on the following day (June 9, 1815) contained this provision:

"The Assembly of the Confederation shall consider methods of bringing about, in a way as uniform as possible, the improvement of the civil status of those who profess the Jewish faith, and, in particular, of securing for them and guaranteeing to them the enjoyment of civic rights in the States of the Confederation, against their accepting all obligations of citizenship."

It was expressly stipulated that the rights which had already been granted to the Jews by various German states would be retained by them.

Minorities in the Balkans

When, in the course of the nineteenth century, Montenegro, Serbia, and Romania followed Greece in achieving their independence from Turkey, these States, as well as Turkey herself, had to guarantee religious freedom and equality of rights irrespective of religion (1878). These freedom and non-discrimination clauses of the Treaty of Berlin of 1878 are the predecessor, not only of the obligations concerning the protection of minorities which were imposed upon a number of States after World War I, but also of the human rights provisions of the Charter of the United Nations.

Prohibition of the Slave Trade

Throughout the nineteenth century, international action was taken aiming at the universal prohibition of the slave trade. In the Peace Treaty of Paris, 1814, France agreed with Britain, without any reservation, that traffic in slaves was "repugnant to the principles of natural justice and of the enlightened age in which we live," and the two States resolved to unite all their efforts "to induce all the Powers of Christendom to decree the abolition of the Slave Trade." The combined English-French effort resulted at the Congress of Vienna (1815) in the signature by the leading European Powers of a "Declaration relative to the Universal Abolition of the Slave Trade." "At length the public voice, in all civilized countries, calls aloud for its prompt suppression," the Declaration states. The Slave Trade was "a scourge which has so long desolated Africa, degraded Europe, and afflicted humanity"; its universal abolition was held to be "a measure particularly worthy of their (the Plenepotentiaries') attention, conformable to the spirit of the times, and to the generous principles of their august sovereigns"; and they resolved to act "with all the zeal and perseverance which is due to so great and noble a cause." The declarants, however, went on to refer to the need for regard "to the interests, the habits, and even the prejudices of their subjects," and to acknowledge that "this general Declaration cannot prejudge the period that each particular Power may consider as most advisable for the definite abolition of the Slave Trade." They concluded that "no proper means of accelerating the attainment of the objective aimed at should be neglected," a sentiment which is still with us in similar connections one and a half centuries later, when as late as in 1926 and even in 1956, it was agreed that slavery and related institutions should be abolished "progressively and as soon as possible." In the Peace Treaty of Paris (1815) the Powers again agreed on taking, without loss of time, "the most effectual measures for the entire and definitive abolition of a commerce so odious, and so strongly condemned by the laws of religion and of nature," an undertaking that was repeated in the Declaration of Verona (1822). In a series of treaties concluded in the following decades, attempts were made to put teeth into the earlier undertakings by vesting the right of visit and search in the naval vessels of the contracting Powers. By the Treaty of Washington, 1862, between the United States and Great Britain, the United States conceded for the first time in a treaty with a foreign Power a right of visit and search over United States' ships suspected of engaging in the slave trade.

In 1885 and 1890, comprehensive and detailed treaty arrangements were made toward the suppression of the slave trade by military, legislative, and economic measures (Berlin Conference, 1885; Brussels Conference, 1890).

In a recent case before the International Court of Justice, one of the Judges identified the abolition of slavery as the beginning of the process of legal advance which in due course led to the promulgation of the Universal Declaration of Human Rights (Judge Bustamente y Rivero, 356).

INTERNATIONAL SOCIAL AND LABOR LEGISLATION

Towards the end of the nineteenth century philanthropists, social reformers, and economists succeeded in arousing interest in, and enlisting the support of some governments for, the idea of international social legislation. A Conference with a large and ambitious program of international measures of social reform convened in Berlin in 1890. The Conference, in spite of an impressive representation from eleven European countries, including the great powers of the day, did not lead to any international agreements. The idea of governments undertaking international obligations in regard to protective labor legislation had hardly, if at all, entered the minds of any statesman of the time except those of Switzerland. The Conference adopted a series of what is called in diplomatic language *"voeux,"* i.e., statements introduced by the phrase "It is desirable . . ." For example: "It is desirable that children of either sex not having reached a certain age be excluded from work in factories, that this limit of age be fixed at twelve years, except for southern countries where the limit may be ten years," or: "It is desirable that girls and women from 16 to 21 years of age should not work at night." Other resolutions covered the question of work in mines, of Sunday labor, and similar problems. In all these *voeux* very liberal facilities for making exceptions were provided. The Berlin Conference of 1890, although generally considered a failure, produced nevertheless an immense moral effect; it attracted attention and made people think. The initiative switched to private individuals and associations. In 1900 the International Association for Labor Legislation, an unofficial body, was formed and it was on the initiative of this association that the first inter-governmental conferences for the conclusion of international labor conventions were held in Berne in 1905, 1906, and 1913. We have here an outstanding example—equaled by few on the international scene— of private initiative, private work, and private ingenuity leading to official international action of considerable magnitude, first, before World War I, within the comparatively limited field of the Berne Conventions of 1906 (to be discussed presently), later, after World War I, within the framework of the International Labor Organization and its multi-faceted activities, and after World War II in the still wider field not only of industrial and labor relations, but of human relations in general, activities which gave expression to the concern of the international community with the protection of human rights for all without distinction as to race, sex, language, and religion.

On September 26, 1906, the second Berne Conference duly adopted two Conventions, the first multi-lateral labor conventions and, I believe, the first multi-lateral international conventions in the wider field of the protection of the human person in history: The International Convention respecting the Prohibition of Night Work for Women in Industrial Employment, and The International Convention respecting the Prohibition of the Use of White (Yellow) Phosphorus in the Manufacture of Matches.

The two conventions were not of equal importance. The Convention prohibiting the employment of women at night affected a very great number of persons. It is estimated that at the time about one million women in twelve industrial States of Europe were affected. The White Phosphorus Convention applied only to a small number of workers who were exposed to the disease of necrosis. It is not the actual provisions of the two conventions, but the principle involved which makes them important. It was their symbolic and moral effect which made them landmarks in the development of modern civilization.

BETWEEN THE TWO GREAT WARS—THE COVENANT OF THE LEAGUE OF NATIONS

Inter arma silent musae; when the arms speak the Muses remain silent, and not only the goddesses of the arts. With the outbreak of World War I in 1914, the question of international labor legislation, like many other peace problems, faded into a remote background.

A Berne Conference of Plenipotentiaries which had been planned for 1914 to put into final shape a series of new international labor conventions, prepared by a conference of experts in the preceding year, could not be held because the prospective contracting parties were by then engaged in a life and death struggle.

The peace treaties by which World War I was ended: the Treaty of Versailles (with Germany), of St. Germain (with Austria), of Trianon (with Hungary), of Neuilly (with Bulgaria), and of Lausanne (with Turkey), and some treaties connected with them, initiated a series of new developments which had a bearing on the relationship between the international community and the rights of individuals and groups. The first four of these treaties contained a part which was the Covenant of the League of Nations.

One of the drafts for the Covenant of the League contained a clause relating to the rights of races and national minorities. In a later draft this stipulation was reduced to a guarantee of the free exercise of religion by religious minorities; but this, too, was later deleted. Japan, one of the victorious powers of World War I, moved for the insertion of a provision which would have obliged the members of the League not to differentiate, in law or in fact, on the ground of race or nationality. The Japanese amendment was not approved, whereupon Japan proposed the insertion of such a provision in the Preamble to the Covenant. This proposal was also defeated and as a result the Covenant, as distinct from its successor, the Charter of the United Nations, did not deal with and recognize the fundamental rights of man and did not contain a provision setting forth the principle of non-discrimination. The Covenant was nevertheless one of the elements in the development towards the international protection of human rights.

In the Covenant the Members of the League accepted the obligation to endeavor to secure and maintain fair and humane conditions of labor for men, women, and children. They undertook to secure the just treatment of the native inhabitants of their colonies. They entrusted the League of Nations with the general supervision over the execution of agreements with regard to the traffic in women and children and pledged themselves to take steps in matters of international concern for the prevention and control of disease. Those of the Powers which had been victorious in World War I and who were entrusted by the League with the tutelage of the colonies and territories which before the War had been governed by Germany and Turkey, accepted, as "a sacred trust of civilization," responsibility for the well-being and development of the peoples concerned. In territories which were deemed not to be sufficiently advanced to be able to administer themselves, the so-called Mandatory Powers had to guarantee freedom of conscience and religion and the prohibition of abuses such as the slave trade.

The Peace Treaties also established the International Labor Organisation of which more will be said below.

THE PROTECTION OF MINORITIES

For our attempt to describe the development of international law towards the recognition of the rights of man in the Charter of the United Nations and the preparation of an international Bill of Human Rights in the post-World War II period, the Treaties and Declarations on the Protection of Minorities, with the League of Nations as guarantor, are of particular interest. In these Treaties and Declarations a number of States of Central and Eastern Europe (Albania, Austria, Bulgaria, Czechoslovakia, Greece, Hungary, Poland, Romania, Yugoslavia, and the Baltic States), and also Iraq, accepted a series of obligations. They undertook to assure full and complete protection of life and liberty to *all inhabitants* without distinction of birth, nationality, language, race, or religion; *all inhabitants* were to be entitled to the free exercise, whether public or private, of any creed, religion, or belief. *All nationals* of the States on which these obligations were imposed were to be equal before the law and were to enjoy the same civil and political rights without distinction as to race, language, or religion. It was provided that differences of religion, creed, or confession shall not prejudice any *national* of the country concerned in matters relating to the enjoyment of civil or political rights, as for instance admission to public employment, functions and honors, or the exercise of professions and industries.

In addition to these provisions which were to apply to *all* inhabitants or to *all* nationals, special stipulations in favor of nationals who belonged to racial, religious, or linguistic minorities were made. Restrictions on the use of any language in private intercourse were prohibited; adequate facilities for the use of the languages of minorities before the courts were guaranteed. The educational needs of linguistic and religious minorities were to be safeguarded. Some of the countries concerned (Poland, Lithuania, and Greece) undertook specific obligations in regard to the religious rights of Jews. Analogous provisions were made for the benefit of Moslems in some Balkan countries and of non-Moslems in Turkey and Iraq.

The system of minorities protection instituted by these instruments had the following characteristics:

(1) The system was not general; it applied only to the states which we have just mentioned. Germany, although defeated, was not among the Powers who had to accept provisions for the protection of their minorities (excepting her obligations towards the population of German Upper Silesia).

(2) The States concerned had to recognize the stipulations of the Treaties as fundamental laws with the effect that no law, regulation, or official action might conflict with them.

(3) The stipulations constituted obligations of international concern, i.e., they were not exclusively domestic matters.

(4) They were placed under the guarantee of the League of Nations. Any Member of the Council of the League could complain of an infraction, or danger of infraction, and in the last re-

sort it was for the World Court in the Hague to settle differences arising from the Treaties.

(5) The members of the minorities themselves had a certain status in the international procedure of supervision. They could present information to the League. Action could, however, be taken only if one or more governments took the matter up.

More specific obligations were undertaken in 1922 by both Germany and Poland for the benefit of the population of Upper Silesia which, after a plebiscite, was divided between those two States.

The question: "Were the Minorities Treaties a Failure?" was carefully studied during World War II. We do not propose to examine it here. It cannot be stated that they ever were a full success; and it cannot be denied that in the thirties they broke down and that an important State bound by one of them (Poland) ceased to co-operate in the implementation of the provisions; Hitler and all that he stood for completed the collapse of the system. As to the question whether the treaties and declarations are still in force after the second World War: it is the prevailing, though not unchallenged, opinion that the fundamental changes that occurred in Central and Eastern Europe and in the Middle East during and after World War II have put an end to their effectiveness. Whether or not they were a failure, whether or not some of them are still in effect, their significance for us and for future generations lies in the fact, that they were an important factor in the process of eroding the concept of absolute State sovereignty in the field of human rights and a telling precedent for international concern with matters which had traditionally been considered as coming within the unfettered discretion of each individual State.

THE INTERNATIONAL LABOR ORGANIZATION

We have already referred to the modest beginnings of what is called "international labor legislation" in the first decade of our century. In this field, too, World War I revolutionized the scene and accelerated developments.

The war was already raging in Europe when the Clayton Act with its celebrated phrase "that the labor of a human being is not a commodity or article of commerce," a provision which was labeled Labor's *Magna Carta,* was enacted in this country on October 15, 1914.

The Clayton Act and its magic phrase has been mentioned here because five years later we are confronted with its replica in the Peace Treaty of Versailles of 1919, where it was stated among the "general principles" that "labor should not be regarded merely as a commodity or article of commerce."*

The Peace Treaty of Versailles established the International Labor Organization and its "Part XIII" became the Constitution of the ILO. The blueprint for the ILO had been prepared by the British and French Governments when the First World War drew to a close, but three Americans played an important part during the negotiations in Paris: Mr. Samuel Gompers (then President of the American Federation of Labor), as chairman of the commission on labor legislation of the Peace Conference, Professor James Shotwell and the then Professor, later Justice of the Supreme Court, Felix Frankfurter. As is well known, the American Senate refused to ratify the Peace Treaty of Versailles and, as a consequence, the United States did not become a member of the League of Nations, nor, initially, of the International Labor Organization. While the United States remained aloof from the League of Nations throughout its existence, it joined the International Labor Organization in 1934.

It would lead us too far to deal in this context with the structure of the International Labor Organization, its history, activities, and achievements. By and large, its aims and methods are the same now, in 1963, as they were laid down in 1919. The aspect which distinguishes the ILO from other international governmental organizations is its "tripartite character," i.e., the fact that States are represented on the International Labor Conference and on the Governing Body of the International Labor Office not only by government delegates, but also by representatives of employers and workers.

The Organization does not have legislative powers in the technical sense of the word. Its Constitution nevertheless confers upon the decisions of the Conference, be they in the form of a Convention or in the form of a Recommendation, more than the

---

*The word "merely" which was added to the American phrase in Versailles was deleted twenty-five years later in the Declaration of Philadelphia of 1944.

status of mere pious wishes. The adoption of a Convention or a Recommendation entails certain legal obligations of Member Governments. The introduction of the idea that the International Labor Conference should have power to make recommendations is due to American initiative and is one of the main contributions of the United States to its Constitution. It was introduced by the American delegation at Versailles to overcome the constitutional difficulties arising from the treaty-making power as regulated in the Constitution of the United States.

Since its establishment in 1919, the International Labor Organization has made a signal contribution to the promotion of human rights through international action not only in fields traditionally comprised by the terms labor law and labor relations, such as industrial health, safety and welfare, hours of work, weekly rest periods, and annual holidays with pay but, particularly after 1945, and in co-operation with the United Nations, also with regard to matters which are at the very core of a system of guarantees of human rights, such as the abolition of forced labor, discrimination in employment and occupation, freedom of association, equal remuneration for work of equal value, and many others.

THE "ENTHRONEMENT OF HUMAN RIGHTS"
AS A PEACE AIM OF WORLD WAR II

The First World War had, in the words of President Wilson, been fought "to make the world safe for democracy," that is "to render it a secure habitation for the fundamental right of man to be governed by rulers chosen by and accountable to him" (Lauterpacht, 77). We have seen that on the conclusion of that war, great strides were made towards this goal. We have also seen, however, that whatever progress had been achieved in 1918 and the years immediately following was wiped out by the horrors of Fascism, National Socialism, and other authoritarian regimes, and by the ordeals of World War II. Hitler's and Mussolini's records proved, moreover, how close a relationship exists between outrageous behavior by a government towards its own subjects and aggression against other nations, between respect for human rights and the maintenance of peace.

This experience resulted in the widespread conviction that the effective international protection of human rights was a major purpose of the war, inasmuch as it is an essential condition of international peace and progress. The first authoritative pronouncement of this aim was made at a time when the United States was not yet at war, in President Roosevelt's Annual Message to the Congress, of January 6, 1941, in which he formulated the Four Freedoms: freedom of speech and expression; freedom of religion; freedom from want; freedom from fear. In the Atlantic Charter of August 14, 1941, the President of the United States (still a neutral) and the Prime Minister of Great Britain expressed the hope "to see established a peace which will afford assurance that all the men in all the lands may live out their lives in freedom from fear and want." In the "Declaration of the United Nations" signed by all the Allied Powers on January 1, 1942, it was stated that "complete victory over their enemies is essential to defend life, liberty, independence, and religious freedom, and to preserve human rights and justice in their own lands as well as in other lands." In a Message to a meeting of protest convened by a Jewish world organization in October, 1942, Prime Minister Winston Churchill spoke of the time "when this world's struggle ends with the enthronement of human rights."

THE DUMBARTON OAKS PROPOSALS

The struggle was by no means over yet when, in the late summer of 1944, the representatives of Britain and the United States met at Dumbarton Oaks, first, with the representatives of the Soviet Union, and later with the representatives of China, and agreed on *"Proposals for the Establishment of a General International Organization"* under the title of *The United Nations.* These "Dumbarton Oaks Proposals" contemplated that the United Nations "should facilitate solutions of international economic, social, and other humanitarian problems and *promote respect for human rights and fundamental freedoms."* When in April, 1945, the representatives of fifty governments assembled at San Francisco to agree upon the final version of the Charter of the United Nations, this reference to human rights and fundamental freedoms was considered inadequate and a certain amount of pressure was brought to bear upon the assembled delegates to broaden the human rights provisions of the Charter.

THE CHARTER OF THE UNITED NATIONS,
SAN FRANCISCO, 1945

As a result, the problem of human rights is referred to in the Preamble and in six different Articles of the Charter. However, what all these provisions, singly and cumulatively, mean has remained controversial up to the present day.

In the Preamble, "the Peoples of the United Nations" express their determination "to reaffirm faith in fundamental human rights, in the dignity and worth of the human person, in the equal rights of men and women and of nations large and small." The words "promoting and encouraging respect for human rights," "assisting in the realization of human rights and fundamental freedoms" appear, with certain variations, in different contexts. The series of provisions on these lines is crowned by two articles in which *"all Members pledge themselves* to take *joint* and *separate* action in co-operation with the Organization for the achievement of a number of purposes which the UN *shall promote,"* among them "universal respect for, and observance of, human rights and fundamental freedoms for all without distinction as to race, sex, language or religion" (Articles 55 and 56).

All these expressions are intentionally vague. When it was proposed at the San Francisco Conference that the United Nations should ensure not only "the *promotion"* but also the *protection* of human rights, the proposal was not accepted. Moreover, a provision was also inserted in the Charter (Art. 2 (7)) which says that nothing in it shall authorize the United Nations to intervene in matters which are essentially within the domestic jurisdiction of any State. This is the often quoted "domestic jurisdiction clause."

As human rights have traditionally come within the domestic jurisdiction of States, it has been concluded by some that the United Nations has no real standing to insist on the safeguarding of human rights in Member States. Moreover, from the vague wording of some of the human rights clauses it has been alleged that by becoming parties to the Charter the Member States have not, in effect, accepted any obligations in the human rights field, that the human rights provisions are not "self-executing" and that, at best, they only express pious hopes and amount to non-enforceable proclamations of principles.

In spite of the restraint exhibited by the authors of the Charter in this matter, it has been claimed by others—and among them were the greatest authorities in international law of that period —that to say that the human rights provisions of the Charter were devoid of any element of legal obligation was no more than a facile generalization; that the provisions of the Charter on the subject figured prominently among the purposes of the United Nations and that the members of the Organization were under a legal obligation to act in accordance with these purposes; that the cumulative legal result of all the pronouncements of the Charter, in particular the "pledge" of Member States, could not be ignored; and that the "domestic jurisdiction clause" did not apply because, as a result of the Charter, human rights had ceased to be "essentially within the domestic jurisdiction of States." Moreover, it has been said that "to intervene" is a technical term of International Law which signifies dictatorial interference and implies peremptory demands. Even if the domestic jurisdiction clause should be held to apply to human rights problems, it would not rule out measures falling short of "intervention." Many hundreds of speeches have been made on this subject within and outside the United Nations by government representatives; thousands of pages of official records have been filled with arguments for and against; hundreds of treatises, books, and articles on either side of the controversy have been devoted to it by learned writers. No purpose would be served if we were to add to this abundance of legal and political arguments.

It can be said, however, that in the actual practice of the various organs of the United Nations over the past seventeen years, the difficulty of solving the apparent contradiction between the "human rights provisions" and the "domestic jurisdiction clause" has been far less formidable than the cleavage of theoretical opinions of scholars and of abstract statements by governments would lead one to assume. In the practice of the United Nations and of its Members, neither the vagueness and generality of the human rights clauses of the Charter, nor the domestic jurisdiction clause have been an obstacle to the United Nations considering, investigating, and judging concrete human rights situations, provided there was a majority strong enough and wishing strongly enough to attempt to influence the particular development.

A cynic might describe the position by saying that governments are usually jealous of the "domestic jurisdiction" of their own and of their allies' and friends' authorities, and that they are far more inclined to assert the jurisdiction of the United Nations when events and developments in other States are involved, particularly in States belonging to the opposite camp in the divided world of our day. Thus, to mention only two examples from the early history of the United Nations: Some governments maintained that the treatment of persons of Indian and Pakistani origin in South Africa, and the racial situation in South Africa as a whole, came within the exclusive domestic jurisdiction of the then Union of South Africa and that, consequently, inquiries into these situations by the United Nations were contrary to the Charter. These same governments had no difficulty in supporting investigations into the alleged existence of forced labor in Eastern Europe, and *vice versa*. As early as 1952-1953 all but two of the then sixty Members of the United Nations were on record as supporting investigations into the race situation in South Africa or the forced labor situation in Eastern Europe, or both. Only South Africa herself and the Perón Government of Argentina had denied to the United Nations the authority to initiate studies and inquiries of this type. As time went on such opposition as had existed against the United Nations taking up issues of this kind weakened, and in some instances disappeared almost entirely, particularly in cases which involved discrimination on the ground of race or color, or colonial problems.

The high-water mark of this development was reached by two decisions taken in the course of the 1963 session of the General Assembly. On October 11, 1963, the Assembly adopted by 106 votes to one (South Africa) a resolution in which it "condemns the Government of the Republic of South Africa for its failure to comply with the repeated resolutions of the General Assembly and of the Security Council calling for an end to the repression of persons opposing *apartheid*," and where, with reference to reports that South Africa is arranging the trial of a large number of political prisoners under arbitrary laws prescribing the death sentence, it requests South Africa "to abandon the arbitrary trial now in progress and forthwith to grant unconditional release to all political prisoners and to all persons imprisoned, interned, or subjected to other restrictions for having opposed the policy of *apartheid.*"

On October 8, 1963, when dealing with the agenda item "The violation of human rights in South Viet-Nam," a non-Member State, the General Assembly agreed, at the invitation of South Viet-Nam, to send a Commission of Member States to make an on-the-spot investigation of the facts of the situation as regarded the alleged violation of Human Rights by the Government of Viet-Nam in its relations with the Buddhist community of that country. The Chairman of the Commission on Human Rights served as chairman of the Mission to South Viet-Nam and the Director of the Division of Human Rights as its Principal Secretary. The task of the Mission, according to its Rules of Procedure, was to seek factual evidence, to collect information, conduct on-the-spot investigations, receive petitions, and hear witnesses. It submitted to the General Assembly a comprehensive report on its fact-finding activities. In view of the changed circumstances (the *coup d'état* in Viet-Nam), the General Assembly considered, in December, 1963, that no further action was required.

Whatever the merits of the opposing contentions as to the interpretation of the Human Rights provisions of the Charter and of its "domestic jurisdiction clause" may be, there was from the beginning general agreement that an International Bill of Human Rights should be prepared in addition to the Human Rights provisions of the Charter. Before we proceed to the examination of United Nations action towards the establishment of an International Bill of Human Rights, it is necessary, however, to mention two developments, which, like the Charter provisions on Human Rights, arose out of World War II: the concept of "crimes against humanity" in connection with the punishment of the war criminals of that war, and the obligations relating to the protection of human rights which the defeated Allies of Germany had to undertake in the Peace Treaties of 1947.

CRIMES AGAINST HUMANITY AND GENOCIDE

"An undisputed gain coming out of Nuremberg is the formal recognition that there are crimes against humanity," said President Truman in November, 1946. What the President commented on was the fact that the Charter of the International Military Tribunal and the Nuremberg Tribunal's judgment in the case against the major German war criminals had meted out punishment not only for war crimes in the technical sense, namely violations of the laws and customs of war, but also for "crimes against humanity" (murder, extermination, enslavement, deportation, and other inhumane acts; persecutions on political, racial, or religious grounds), "committed against any civilian population," i.e., including German citizens, "whether or not in violation of the domestic law of the country where perpetrated," meaning that murderous Nazi "laws" were no defense. The Nuremberg Tribunal applied a cautious and restrictive approach to this "revolution in international criminal law." Nevertheless the treatment by a State and by its organs of the State's own citizens was made the subject of criminal proceedings in a court which functioned as an organ of the international community. This established an important principle and an inroad into the traditional concepts of absolute sovereignty and its corollary: exclusive domestic jurisdiction. The principles on which the Nuremberg Tribunal acted were subsequently endorsed by the General Assembly and are to be embodied in a "Code of Offenses Against the Peace and Security of Mankind."

The Genocide Convention, which was adopted in 1948 and to which most States of the world (though not the United States and Britain) are parties, is closely connected with the principles of Nuremberg. In the Genocide Convention the Contracting Parties have confirmed that genocide, whether committed in time of peace or in time of war, is a crime under international law which they undertake to prevent and to punish. Genocide means certain acts committed "with intent to destroy, in whole or in part, a national, ethnical, racial, or religious group as such." Genocide, even if perpetrated by a government in its own territory against its own citizens, is not, as far as the States Parties to the Convention are concerned, a matter essentially within the domestic jurisdiction of States, but a matter of international concern.

HUMAN RIGHTS IN THE PEACE TREATIES OF 1947

In the Treaties of Peace with Italy, Romania, Bulgaria, Hungary, and Finland, these former enemy States undertook to "take all measures necessary to secure to all persons under their jurisdiction, without distinction as to race, sex, language, or religion, the enjoyment of human rights and of the fundamental freedoms, including freedom of expression, of press and publication, of religious worship, of political opinion and of public meetings." A provision to the same effect was also included in the State Treaty with Austria of 1955. Hungary, Romania, and Austria further had to undertake that the laws in force shall not, either in their content or in their application, discriminate or entail any discrimination between the citizens of these States "on the ground of their race, sex, language, or religion, whether in reference to their persons, property, business, professional, or financial interests, status, political or civil rights, or any other matter." In view of their record it was not considered necessary to impose a similar anti-discrimination provision on Bulgaria, Finland, and Italy. All the Treaties with the six countries contain provisions for the settlement of disputes concerning their interpretation or execution. Such disputes are, in the last resort, to be decided by an arbitral tribunal whose decisions are definitive and binding. Thus the six Treaties contain "Bills of Rights" with international "Measures of Implementation," terms we propose to explain presently. As will be seen later, these arrangements which looked perfect on paper broke down, however, when put to the test.

THE INTERNATIONAL BILL OF RIGHTS

At the San Francisco Conference which drafted the Charter of the United Nations in 1945, a proposal to embody an International Bill of Rights in the Charter itself was put forward but not proceeded with for the reason that it required more detailed consideration. The idea of establishing an International Bill of Rights was, however, treated as inherent in the Charter. Even before the Charter was ratified and before it entered into force and before the United Nations as an organization was established, steps were taken towards this goal. The "Preparatory Commission of the United Nations" and its "Executive Committee," meeting in the Autumn of 1945, both recommended that the work of the Commission on Human Rights, the establishment of which is provided for in the Charter, should be directed, in the first place, towards the "formulation of an international bill of rights." The General Assembly agreed with these recommendations in January, 1946. Accordingly, when the terms of reference of the

Commission on Human Rights were laid down in February, 1946, "an international bill of rights" was the first item on its work program. When the Commission and a drafting committee which had been established started their work on this ambitious project, it turned out that there was doubt and disagreement among the members about the form which the draft Bill of Rights should take. Some members thought the Bill should be a "declaration" or "manifesto" which would be proclaimed by a resolution of the General Assembly. Others urged that it should take the form of an international treaty which, in addition to being approved by the General Assembly, would have to be opened for signature, ratification, and accession by governments to be binding only on those governments which had ratified it or acceded to it. The relevant report of the Drafting Committee records that it was agreed by those who favored the Declaration form that the Declaration should be accompanied or followed by one or more Conventions. It was also agreed by those who favored the Convention form that the General Assembly in recommending a Convention to Member Nations might make a Declaration wider in content or more general in expression. As a consequence, drafts of a "Declaration" and of a "Convention" were prepared and studies were also undertaken for the creation of international supervisory and enforcement machinery, usually styled "measures of implementation."

At the end of 1947 the Commission on Human Rights arrived at a decision to solve this basic controversy in the following way. It decided:

(1) To apply the term "International Bill of Human Rights," or, for brevity, "Bill of Rights" to the entirety of documents in preparation: the Declaration, the Convention, and the Measures of Implementation;

(2) To present a separate draft of the "Declaration";

(3) To call the Convention on Human Rights which it had prepared "The Covenant on Human Rights"; and

(4) To refer to the outcome of various suggestions for international supervision as "Measures of Implementation," regardless of whether these measures will eventually form part of the Covenant or not.

In 1948 the Commission on Human Rights submitted to its superior bodies, the Economic and Social Council and the General

Assembly, the draft Declaration which it had prepared. It also forwarded the draft covenant prepared by its drafting committee. It added that further work on the question of implementation was of the utmost importance and that it would embark upon this work at its next session. The General Assembly which received all three drafts at its session held in Paris in the Autumn of 1948 decided to consider only the Draft Declaration, as the other two documents (the Covenant and Measures of Implementation) were not yet in a state suitable for consideration. After long and protracted discussions in one of its Main Committees and in meetings of the plenary Assembly, the General Assembly made definite and final the division of the "International Bill of Human Rights" into its component parts.

On December 10, 1948 it adopted and proclaimed the Universal Declaration of Human Rights by forty-eight votes for, none against, and eight abstentions. At the same time it decided that work relating to the draft Covenant on Human Rights and draft Measures of Implementation should continue and should be given priority.

The draft Covenant on Human Rights and the Measures of Implementation are not the subject of this little book. It must be sufficient therefore to say here that it was subsequently decided that there should be two Covenants, one on civil and political rights, the other on economic, social, and cultural rights, and that either Covenant should contain the measures of implementation appropriate to its subject matter. At the time of writing (Summer, 1963), the Assembly's work relating to the two draft Covenants has not yet been completed, although slow but considerable progress has been made.

We shall now proceed to an examination of the Universal Declaration of Human Rights, that part of the International Bill of Rights which has now been in existence for fifteen years.

PART TWO

The Growth

THE UNIVERSAL DECLARATION OF HUMAN RIGHTS — 1948 TO 1963

The Universal Declaration of Human Rights owes its existence to the decision taken in 1947-1948 to produce the International Bill of Rights not by one single, comprehensive, and final act, but to divide it into at least two, but probably more, international instruments of which the Universal Declaration of Human Rights would be the first. This was, of course, a compromise solution by which the General Assembly, at its 1948 session, concentrated on that part of the Bill on which agreement could be achieved without insurmountable political, ideological, and technical difficulties. The promulgation, on December 10, 1948, of the Universal Declaration, coupled with the delay of the completion of the International Bill of Rights has created a situation which is not free from difficulties. Many of those who prepared and supported the Universal Declaration and who voted for it did not anticipate that during its existence as the sole completed part of the International Bill of Human Rights the instrument would exert an influence far beyond its authors' intentions.

Moreover, events which took place in the fifteen years since December 10, 1948, have profoundly modified the constitutional set-up of the United Nations, have transformed the international scene with an intensity undreamed of in 1948, and have as a consequence changed the place of the Declaration in the scheme of things.

The status of the Declaration has been controversial from its very beginning. The statements of its drafters and of the governments of the time on its constitutional, legal, political, and moral value reflected a great variety of views in 1948. Even then it was a very difficult undertaking to analyze both the Declaration as a whole and its individual provisions with the hope that one's opinions would remain uncontested and would be generally agreed to. Today, in 1963, after so many events which could not fail to affect the Declaration and its status, it is completely impossible to present an evaluation which will be generally accepted as the only correct one. The reader is warned, therefore, that the observations that follow are based on the author's own opinions. These are sincerely held. They are the result of an analysis of the facts and events as he sees them. It is hoped that the conclusion will be agreed to by decision-makers and scholars alike; but the author does not wish to present them, at the present stage at least, as a generally accepted interpretation of the relevant provisions and of the bearing which subsequent events have had upon them.

THE DECLARATION AS A RESOLUTION
OF THE GENERAL ASSEMBLY

The Declaration is that part of the International Bill of Rights which is not in the form of an international convention or treaty. This is why it has been claimed that the Declaration does not involve a contractual obligation of governments to guarantee the rights set forth in it; this is also why it was more readily acceptable to governments than a treaty possessed of coercive power would have been. It must also be admitted, at the outset, that the Declaration is studiously vague and ambiguous on the very basic questions of its own validity and status. Under the constitutional arrangements as contemplated in the United Nations Charter, the General Assembly, from which the Universal Declaration emanates, is not supposed to be a legislative body and the force attributed to its pronouncements is generally considered to be that of "recommendations."

Was the Declaration meant to be a "recommendation"? The word "recommendation" does not appear in the whole instrument. The Declaration describes itself as "a common understanding" of the rights and freedoms which the Members of the United Nations have "pledged themselves" in the Charter to promote. This would appear to mean that, in adopting the Declaration, the Member States have agreed on the nature and scope of the rights

35

and freedoms which they are already under a duty to respect, a duty or "pledge" which calls for "full realization." On the other hand, the General Assembly proclaimed the Declaration as "a common standard of achievement," i.e., something that is not yet realized but should be aimed at in the near, or more distant, future. The Preamble to the Declaration does not say what States should do. As a matter of fact, States as such are not mentioned in it at all. The Declaration is addressed to "every individual and every organ of society" who, "keeping this Declaration constantly in mind, shall strive by teaching and education to promote respect for these rights and freedoms and by progressive measures, national and international, to secure their universal and effective recognition and observance." States are, of course, "organs of society." State legislation comes within the notion of "measures."

On the same day the General Assembly adopted the Declaration it *recommended* to Governments in a different resolution to show their adherence to Article 56 of the Charter (i.e., the Charter provision containing the "pledge") by publicizing and disseminating the Declaration. Are the provisions of the Declaration then recommendations addressed to Member States, or has the Assembly simply recommended that the States publicize and disseminate them? To put this question is tantamount to replying to it. If all the General Assembly wanted Governments to do was to disseminate the Declaration, surely it could not have—in the same breath, as it were—stated that "the adoption of the Universal Declaration of Human Rights is an historic act, destined to consolidate world peace through the contribution towards the liberation of individuals from the unjustified oppression and constraint to which they are too often subjected." Fourteen years later, in 1962, the General Assembly stated in a resolution making arrangements for the commemoration of the fifteenth anniversary of the Declaration in 1963, that "notwithstanding some progress, the situation regarding compliance *with the recommendations made in the Declaration* remains unsatisfactory in many parts of the world." The correct view is therefore probably that in 1948 the Declaration, in spite of the studiously vague language of its Preamble, was a recommendation and, at the same time, more than that.

It would have been a rather daring statement to assert then that the Declaration was a legally binding instrument. The author believes, however, that this negative judgment must now be somewhat qualified.

THE DEVELOPMENT SINCE 1948

In the years since 1948 the Universal Declaration has acquired a purpose different from the one which was contemplated and willed by many of the governments that brought it into being in 1948. This change did not originate in the document which did not, and could not, of its own accord, as it were, transform its mission, its function and its legal status. It was the international community, the States which had been instrumental in its creation as well as those which acceded to independence after that time, that used the Declaration for the purpose of fulfilling an assignment greater and more far-reaching than that which had been originally carved out for it. Not as the result of a methodical legislative process, but through unplanned, haphazard action, have governments and inter-governmental organizations, courts and legislatures invested the Declaration with an increased and increasing authority and practical importance.

What has taken place has been the operation of a fundamental law of physics: nature abhors a vacuum. The process of creating an international law of human rights by the traditional method of concluding international treaties, by establishing and putting into force the world-wide "international covenants on human rights" has slowed down. As a consequence the Declaration has, temporarily at least, filled the void. The Declaration took over the function originally contemplated for the International Bill of Rights as a whole. The Declaration of 1948 was followed by a series of other declarations created through the same process. In a period when the conclusion of international treaties has—temporarily it is hoped—become unavailable as a method of achieving universal progress in our divided world, the less orthodox method of agreeing upon "declarations" has been resorted to and the Universal Declaration of 1948 has been reinforced, one might almost say, re-enacted in the process. In the following pages, we shall describe this fascinating and, in the truest sense of the word, revolutionary process. This will reveal the fact that twelve years after 1948, when the "Declaration on the Granting of Independence to Colonial Countries and Peoples" of 1960 came into being, the status of the Declaration of 1948 had already been enhanced to such an extent that it was laid down that "All states *shall observe faithfully and strictly* the provisions of the Charter of the United Nations, *the Universal Declaration of Human Rights* and the present Declaration...." (i.e., the Declaration of 1960).

THE DECLARATION AS A YARDSTICK OF
THE OBSERVANCE OF HUMAN RIGHTS

No sooner had the Declaration been adopted when it started to be used as a code of conduct and as a yardstick to measure the compliance by Governments with the international standards of human rights. The first instance occurred as early as April, 1949, when a complaint was brought before the General Assembly that the Soviet Union had violated fundamental human rights and other principles of the United Nations Charter by preventing Soviet wives of citizens of other nationalities from leaving their countries with their husbands or in order to join them abroad. The General Assembly invoked the articles of the Declaration which provide that everyone has the right to leave any country including his own and that men and women of full age have the right to marry without any limitation due to race, nationality or religion. It declared that the measures taken by the Soviet Union were not in conformity with the Charter and it called upon the Government of the U.S.S.R. to withdraw them.

Another human rights conflict which came before the General Assembly early in its history was the treatment of people of Indian and Pakistani origin in South Africa. In repeated resolutions the General Assembly exhorted the parties to solve the dispute on the basis of the provisions of the Charter and of the Declaration. On the question of the racial situation in South Africa, an issue which is still before the United Nations, the Assembly repeatedly invoked the Declaration in its endeavor to have South Africa abandon the policy of racial discrimination. In countless other disputes and controversies which it was called upon to examine, the United Nations and its various organs had recourse to the Declaration, whether they were dealing with allegations of forced labor, discrimination in Non-Self-Governing and Trust Territories, with the situation in Tibet, or in South West Africa, with customs and practices inconsistent with the physical integrity and dignity of women and with many other blemishes of our civilization. The Universal Declaration has played a great role also in the activities of Specialized Agencies such as the International Labor Organization, UNESCO and the Universal Telecommunication Union, in regional organizations such as the Organization of American States and the Council of Europe, at the Bandung Conference of Asian-African States of 1955 and in many other contexts and on many other occasions. The important provisions relating to the Declaration and included in the Constitution of the Organization of African Unity (1963) are described later in this book.

The Universal Declaration and the Encyclical "Pacem in Terris"

This booklet concentrates on describing the role which governments and organizations of governments have played in the elaboration and proclamation of the Universal Declaration of Human Rights and the impact of the Declaration on States and organizations of States and on international and constitutional law. It is nevertheless appropriate to refer here also to the authoritative views relating to the Declaration expressed in an historic document issued in the year of the Declaration's fifteenth anniversary: the Encyclical *"Pacem in Terris"* (Peace on Earth) of the late Pope John XXIII (April 11, 1963). As it would lead us too far to describe here in detail the extent to which the Encyclical supports most of the concrete provisions of the Declaration and, in general, the human rights program of the United Nations, we must limit ourselves to quoting the Pope's statements that the proclamation of the Declaration by the General Assembly was "an act of the highest importance" and that "there is no doubt that the document represents an important step on the path towards the juridical-political organization of the world community. For in it, in most solemn form, the dignity of a person is acknowledged to all human beings; and as a consequence there is proclaimed, as a fundamental right, the right of free movement in the search for truth and in the attainment of moral good and of justice, and also the right to a dignified life."

THE DECLARATION AND
INTERNATIONAL CONVENTIONS

Comprehensive Conventions

The Declaration, it is said, started its career as a "non-binding pronouncement" to be followed by the "binding" part of the International Bill of Rights, the Covenant, or Covenants, on Human Rights and Measures of Implementation. The Covenants have not yet materialized, but to some extent substitute arrangements have been made in various ways. The countries of Western Europe, Members of the Council of Europe, transformed most of the provisions of the Declaration into traditional, "binding," conventional law by agreeing upon and putting into effect the "Convention for the Protection of Human Rights and Fundamental Freedoms" signed in Rome on November 4, 1950, supplemented by Protocols of 1952 and 1963 and, as far as economic and social rights are concerned, by the European Social Charter of 1961. It is the purpose of the Rome Convention "to take the first steps for the collective enforcement of certain of the Rights stated in the Universal Declaration" which "aims at securing the universal and effective recognition and observance of the Rights therein declared." To the European Convention on Human Rights belongs a place of distinction among the international instruments designed to bring about the legal protection of human rights on the international level. It is the most advanced instrument in this field. It has created a European Commission on Human Rights which has jurisdiction to consider complaints by States Parties of the non-observance of the rights set forth in the Convention. With regard to the majority of the Parties, it can also consider complaints lodged by individuals. A European Court of Human Rights has also been established. These institutions take the place, in Western Europe, of the organs which, if the completion of the Draft Covenants on Human Rights had not been delayed, would be in existence on a world-wide basis. Similar institutions are contemplated for the Americas. (Draft Convention on Human Rights, Inter-American Commission for the Protection of Human Rights, Inter-American Court of Human Rights.)

While the European Convention and Social Charter and the planned Inter-American Convention cover, roughly, the substance, i.e., the various rights set forth in the Declaration, they are, of course, not world-wide in scope but apply, or will apply, only in the specific regions of Western Europe and of the Americas.

Conventions on Specific Subjects

In contrast, there have come into being a series of international conventions, all prepared by the United Nations or its specialized agencies, which, while of a world-wide character, are restricted to certain aspects of human rights, to specific, often narrow problems. They do not cover the entire ground.

In the course of the year 1948, at the end of which, on December 10, the Universal Declaration on Human Rights was proclaimed, several international conventions in the human rights field were adopted, two of which are of particular importance. One of them is the Convention on the Prevention and Punishment of the Crime of Genocide, adopted by the General Assembly on December 9, 1948, to which reference has already been made. The other is the Freedom of Association and Protection of the Right to Organize Convention, adopted by the International Labor Conference in June/July, 1948.

Freedom of Association. Article 20 of the Universal Declaration provides (1) that everyone has the right to peaceful assembly and association, and (2) that no one may be compelled to belong to an association. In addition, the Declaration contains a specific provision relating to trade unions, Art. 23 (4), which is to the effect that everyone has the right to form and to join trade unions for the protection of his interest. It is doubtful whether the provision of Article 20 (2) applies to trade unions.

The Freedom of Association Convention, adopted by the International Labor Conference a few months before December 10, 1948, is one of the first world-wide Conventions to deal with a fundamental human right. "Workers and Employers," it provides, "without distinction whatsoever, shall have the right to establish and, subject only to the rules of the organization concerned, to join organizations of their own choosing without previous authorization" (Art. 2). The organizations "shall have the right to draw up their constitutions and rules, to elect their representatives in full freedom . . . and to formulate their programmes. The public authorities shall refrain from any interference which would restrict this right or impede the lawful exercise thereof" (Art. 3). In exercising these rights "workers and employers and their respective organizations, like other persons or organized collectivities, shall respect the law of the land." However: "The law of the land shall not be such as to impair, nor shall it be so applied as to impair, the guarantees provided in this Convention" (Art. 8).

Right to a Nationality. Article 15 of the Declaration provides that everyone has the right to a nationality and that no one shall be arbitrarily deprived of his nationality nor denied the right to change his nationality. This is clearly one of the weakest provisions of the Declaration, the second sentence being contradictory to the first. If a State is permitted to deprive a person of his nationality provided that the deprivation does not take place "arbitrarily," then the person concerned loses his right to the nationality he holds and is by no means assured of the acquisition of another. Efforts to abolish the evil of statelessness "which is a stigma upon international law and a challenge to human dignity in an international legal system in which nationality is the main link between the individual and international law" (Lauterpacht, 423), have so far not proved successful. A draft Convention on the Elimination of Future Statelessness, drafted in 1953 and 1954, did not commend itself to governments and, in 1961, a convention with the much more modest aim of a *"reduction* of statelessness" was signed by a number of governments. The Convention of 1961, although it does not, even among States which become Parties to it, achieve the aim of guaranteeing to everyone the right to a nationality, is of special interest to us also because one of its provisions incorporates Articles 13 and 14 of the Declaration which deal with freedom of movement, the right to leave any country (including one's own) and to return to one's country, and the right to seek asylum.

One aspect of the "right to a nationality" has been implemented by the United Nations Convention on the Nationality of Married Women of 1957, in which each Contracting State agrees that neither the celebration nor the dissolution of marriage between one of its nationals and an alien shall automatically affect the nationality of the wife.

While efforts to eliminate statelessness failed, action was taken to alleviate the plight of stateless persons and of refugees who are not stateless, by the conclusion of conventions on the status of refugees (1951) and of stateless persons (1954), the basic principles of which are: first, that there should be as little discrimination as possible between nationals on the one hand and refugees or stateless persons on the other; second, that there should be no discrimination at all based on race, religion, or country of origin among refugees and among stateless persons.

Political Rights. "Everyone has the right to take part in the government of his country, directly or through freely chosen representatives," provides Article 21 of the Declaration. This provision has been made the basis of the Convention on the Political Rights of Women of 1952. It is to the effect that women shall be entitled to vote in all elections to all publicly elected bodies, and that they shall be entitled to hold public office and to exercise all public functions, all this on equal terms with men and without any discrimination.

Slavery and Forced Labor. We have already seen that the combatting of slavery and the slave trade has been one of the aims of international humanitarian endeavor since the beginning of the nineteenth century. The Universal Declaration continues the struggle. Its Article 4 provides that no one shall be held in slavery or servitude; slavery and the slave trade shall be prohibited in all their forms. It was not necessary to build from scratch in this field as prohibitions of both slavery and forced labor had been made the subject of detailed international regulations in the period between the two wars. In 1926 a Slavery Convention was concluded under the auspices of the League of Nations. In 1956, a Supplementary Convention on the Abolition of Slavery, the Slave Trade, and Institutions and Practices similar to Slavery was concluded. The contribution made by this Convention consists in the outlawing of certain institutions and practices similar to slavery, such as debt bondage, serfdom, purchase of brides, and exploitation of child labor. In the following year, by the Convention concerning the Abolition of Forced Labor, 1957, States undertook to suppress and not to make use of any form of forced or compulsory labor, *inter alia,* as a means of political coercion or education or as a punishment for holding or expressing political views or views ideologically opposed to the established political, social, or economic system; as a method of mobilizing or using labor for purposes of economic development; or as a means of racial, social, national, or religious discrimination.

In July, 1963, President Kennedy submitted the three Conventions mentioned in this and in the preceding paragraph, i.e., the Political Rights of Women Convention of 1952, the Supplementary Slavery Convention of 1956, and the Forced Labor Convention of 1957, to the United States Senate for advice and consent to their ratification.

Free Consent to Marriage. Article 16 (2) of the Declaration provides that marriage shall be entered into only with the free and full consent of the intending spouses. On December 10, 1962, Human Rights Day, a Convention was signed in which more precise provisions regulating this problem are given. No marriage shall be legally entered into, this most recent Human Rights Convention provides, without the full and free consent of both parties, such consent to be expressed by them in person after due publicity and in the presence of the Authority competent to solemnize the marriage and of witnesses as prescribed by law. State parties shall specify a minimum age for marriage. All marriages shall be registered.

Prohibition of Discrimination. If we try to establish the most basic principle which underlies the Universal Declaration of Human Rights and the whole system of the protection of human rights which has been erected by the United Nations family of organizations, we find that it is the principle of non-discrimination. The Charter itself which, in other respects, does not define the human rights and fundamental freedoms the promotion of which it has made one of the purposes of the United Nations, repeatedly emphasizes one aspect: that the United Nations is here to assist in the realization of human rights and fundamental freedoms *for all* and *without distinction* as to *race, sex, language,* or *religion.* The Declaration proclaims "the *equal* and inalienable rights of *all members of the human family."* It declares that "All human beings are born free *and equal* in dignity and rights" (Art. 1). It goes on to provide that *"Everyone* is entitled to all the rights and freedoms set forth in this Declaration, *without distinction of any kind, such as race, color, sex, language, religion, political or other opinion, national or social origin, property, birth or other status"* (Art. 2). It anticipates the revolutionary rising of dependent peoples by adding that "no distinction shall be made on the basis of the political, jurisdictional, or international status of the country or territory to which a person belongs, whether it be independent, trust, non-self-governing, or under any other limitation of sovereignty" (Art. 2 [2]). Article 7 of the Declaration provides: "All are equal before the law and are entitled without any discrimination to equal protection of the law. All are entitled to equal protection against any discrimination in violation of this Declaration and against any incitement to such discrimination." The principle of non-discrimination permeates the Declaration to such an extent that throughout the instrument all positive rights are attributed to "everyone" (e.g., "everyone has the right to life, liberty and security of person," "everyone has the right to an effective remedy," "everyone is entitled in full equality to a fair and public hearing"), and the prohibitions are formulated in such a way that "no one" must be subjected to the prohibited treatment (e.g., "no one shall be held in slavery or servitude," "no one shall be subjected to torture or to cruel inhuman or degrading treatment or punishment," "no one shall be subjected to arbitrary arrest, detention or exile," "no one shall be arbitrarily deprived of his property").

Two very basic aspects of the problem of discrimination have been made the subject of regulation by international conventions. These are the result of the co-operation between the United Nations and the International Labor Organization and UNESCO respectively: discrimination in employment and discrimination in education.

The Discrimination (Employment and Occupation) Convention, 1958. By this Convention, each State Party undertakes to declare and pursue a national policy designed to promote equality of opportunity and treatment in respect of employment and occupation, with a view to eliminating any discrimination in respect thereof.

Contracting States also undertake by methods appropriate to national conditions and practice, *inter alia,* to enact such legislation as may be calculated to secure the acceptance and observance of the policy and to repeal any statutory provisions and modify any administrative instructions or practices which are inconsistent with the policy. Earlier, in 1951, the *Equal Renumeration Convention* had given enhanced status in international law to the old *desideratum* of the women's movement, proclaimed in Article 23 (2) of the Declaration: "Everyone, without any discrimination, has the right to equal pay for equal work," and also recognized as a principle in the Peace Treaty of Versailles and in the revised constitution of the International Labor Organization.

The Convention Against Discrimination in Education, 1960.
This convention, concluded under the auspices of UNESCO, is
the counterpart, in the educational field, to the Discrimination
(Employment and Occupation) Convention, 1958, which had
been worked out by the International Labor Organization.

We cannot deal here with the very comprehensive provisions
of the 1960 Convention which go to the root of the problem in its
many ramifications. It outlaws, among other things, "depriving
any person or group of persons of access to education of any type
or at any level"; "limiting any person or group of persons to education of an inferior standard"; "inflicting on any person or group
of persons conditions which are incompatible with the dignity of
man"; "establishing or maintaining separate educational systems
or institutions for persons or groups of persons." From the last-
mentioned prohibition the Convention permits certain exceptions but only subject to strict conditions. It permits, e.g., the establishment or maintenance of separate educational systems or
institutions for pupils of the two sexes if they offer equivalent access to education, provide a teaching staff with qualifications of
the same standard as well as school premises and equipment of
the same quality, and afford the opportunity to take the same or
equivalent courses of study. The States Parties also undertake to
ensure that there is no discrimination in the admission of pupils
to educational institutions; not to allow any differences of treatment by the public authorities, except on the basis of merit or
need, in the matter of school fees, scholarships etc.; not to allow,
in any form of assistance granted by the public authorities to educational institutions, any restrictions or preference based solely
on the ground that pupils belong to a particular group. The
States undertake to direct their national policy towards making
primary education free and compulsory; to make secondary education in its different forms generally available and accessible to
all and to make higher education equally accessible to all on the
basis of individual capacity.

THE PENETRATION OF THE DECLARATION
INTO CONVENTIONAL INTERNATIONAL LAW

The impact of the Declaration on conventional international
law is not exhausted by its having been the basis for the conclu-

sion and coming into force of the various special conventions in the fields of nationality and statelessness, political rights, slavery, forced labor, marriage, and the combatting of discrimination in employment and in education. The various conventions embody, mostly in their Preambles, references to the Declaration as such. Thus in the Convention on the Political Rights of Women of 1952 the States Parties recognize that everyone has the right to take part in the government of his country; in the Marriage Convention of 1962 they also endorse the provision of Article 16 (1) of the Declaration which provides that men and women of full age, without any limitation due to race, nationality or religion, have the right to marry and to found a family and that they are entitled to equal rights as to marriage, during marriage and at its dissolution. In the same Convention, the States Parties reaffirm that all States should take all appropriate measures to ensure complete freedom in the choice of a spouse. The Convention on the Nationality of Married Women of 1957 endorses Article 15 of the Declaration on the right to a nationality; the 1958 Convention on Discrimination in Employment and Occupation states, quite generally, that discrimination constitutes a *violation of rights* enunciated in the Declaration and the 1960 Convention against Discrimination in Education states the same about discrimination in education. The 1957 Convention on Forced Labor similarly establishes that certain forms of forced or compulsory labor constitute *a violation of the rights of man* referred to in the Charter and enunciated by the Declaration. The natural and ordinary meaning of the phrase "violation of rights" indicates that we are confronted with clauses which operate in the sphere of law, that the rights set forth in the Declaration are legal rights and that it can no longer be maintained, whatever the position may have been in 1948, that the Declaration has "only moral force."

New Comprehensive International Instruments Against Racial Discrimination

In 1962 the General Assembly made arrangements for the preparation of a Declaration and of a Convention "on the elimination of all forms of racial discrimination." The Declaration on that subject was adopted and proclaimed on November 20, 1963.

It will be found in Appendix II to this book. It is envisaged that a draft international convention on the elimination of all forms of racial discrimination will be before the General Assembly at its session in 1964.

So far we have dealt with the penetration of the Declaration into positive, conventional International Law through various treaties, world-wide and regional, the main and only purpose of which was the protection of specific rights or groups of rights. To round out the picture we shall now refer to a series of instances where the Universal Declaration of Human Rights was made an element in the settlement of post-war political problems.

The Japanese Peace Treaty

In the Preamble to the Peace Treaty with Japan, signed at San Francisco in 1951, the following two paragraphs occur:

> "Whereas Japan for its part, declares its intention . . . to strive to realize the objectives of the Universal Declaration of Human Rights. . . .
> Whereas the Allied Powers welcome the intention of Japan as described in the preceding paragraph. . . ."

These statements are in dialogue form, as it were. The first records a declaration of intention on the part of Japan, the second the welcoming of this intention on the part of the victorious Allied Powers. On its face, the text records a meeting of minds, one of the normal elements of a contract or treaty. Accordingly, when the Prime Minister of Japan reported to the Japanese Diet on the signature of the Peace Treaty, he spoke of the references to human rights which we have just quoted as of "basic stipulations" of the treaty, which had been put in the form of a voluntary declaration. An examination of the records of the Peace Conference shows, however, that it had not been the intention of the leading Allied Power, the United States, to impose on Japan legal obligations in respect of human rights. When the Japanese Peace Treaty was submitted to the United States Senate for consent to ratification in 1952, it provoked criticism because of the reference in the Preamble to the objectives of the Universal Declaration. Influential Senators do not view treaties on human rights favorably even when the party accepting an obligation in this regard is not the United States, but its former enemy. For this reason the Department of State, in a memorandum circulated to the Senate, stressed the fact that the Peace Treaty did not impose a legal obligation on Japan to respect human rights. There arose therefore the strange situation that Japan, the nation being the "promisor" in this relationship, gladly and without opposition, considered the text as a stipulation, while the United States, the leading "promisee" nation, the most influential member of the victorious coalition, allowed its allergy to "treaty coercion" in the matter of human rights to lead it to the assertion that the treaty did not impose obligations in the matter of human rights on its defeated enemy.

Trieste

At the conclusion of World War II, the harbor city of Trieste and its surroundings were a bone of contention between Italy and Yugoslavia. The Peace Treaty with Italy of 1947 attempted to solve the controversy by establishing the "Free Territory of Trieste" as an entity separate from both Italy and Yugoslavia. However, the Great Powers could not agree on the appointment of a Governor for Trieste and the Free Territory has never become a going concern although, under the Peace Treaty, it has existed on paper. In 1954, Italy and Yugoslavia, in co-operation with the United States and Britain, and with the acquiescence of the Soviet Union, proceeded to divide the territory and to place its Northern part under Italian, its Southern part under Yugoslav, administration. At the same time Italy and Yugoslavia agreed upon a "Special Statute" for both parts of the territory in which they undertook to guarantee to all inhabitants of the two areas without discrimination the full enjoyment of the fundamental rights and freedoms laid down in the Universal Declaration of Human Rights. This was the first case where, through international agreement, the provisions of the Declaration in their totality have been made to apply in a certain territory. The Special Statute also contains provisions for the protection of the Yugoslav and Italian minorities in the two areas which go beyond the provisions of the Declaration. The Special Statute of 1954 also provides for the establishment of a special mixed Yugoslav-Italian committee which is authorized to examine complaints and questions raised by individuals belonging to the respective ethnic groups concerning the implementation of the Statute.*

THE DECLARATION IN AFRICA

Former Trust Territories

Somaliland. When, in 1950, Italy was entrusted with the administration of its former colony of Somaliland as a United Nations Trust Territory, she accepted, in the Trusteeship Agreement, the Universal Declaration of Human Rights "as a standard of achievement." When, ten years later, Somaliland under Italian Trusteeship, joined by British Somaliland, achieved independence, as the Republic of Somalia, a provision was inserted in its Constitution to the effect that the new state shall adopt "as far as applicable" the provisions of the Declaration. "As far as applicable" is, of course, a very substantial qualification.

Togoland and the Cameroons. When, in 1956, Togoland under French Administration was preparing for independence—which it achieved in 1960—it received a "Statute of the Autonomous Republic of Togoland" providing that laws issuing from its legislature must be in conformity with, among other things, the principles set forth in the Universal Declaration of Human Rights. Laws repugnant to the Declaration were deemed to be unconstitutional and could be declared invalid. The provisions relating to the Universal Declaration of Human Rights introduced in the French Cameroons in 1957 were similar in character.

The Constitution of the Independent Republic of Togo of 1961 proclaims in its Preamble the firm attachment of its people to the principles which have inspired the Universal Declaration of Human Rights. An affirmation of its adherence to the fundamental liberties inscribed in the Universal Declaration of Human Rights and in the Charter of the United Nations is also contained in the Constitution of the Federal Republic of Cameroon adopted in the same year (1961).

The Universal Declaration in Other African Constitutions

The first African State to embody its endorsement of the United Nations Charter and of the Universal Declaration in its Con-

---

*For difficulties which have arisen in the implementation of the Statute see below.

stitution was the Republic of Guinea (1958). Eleven other African States which had formerly been French colonies followed suit by expressing their adherence to the Declaration in the Preambles to their Constitutions: Chad, Congo (Brazzaville), Ivory Coast, Dahomey, Gabon, Madagascar, Mali, Mauritania, Niger, Senegal, and Upper Volta.

The Constitution of the Kingdom of *Burundi*, which, until 1962, had been part of the Belgian Trust Territory of Ruanda-Urundi, affirms in the Preamble the King's belief in God and his faith in the high dignity of the human person and his decision to guarantee fundamental human rights, and records that he takes his inspiration from the Universal Declaration of Human Rights and from the Charter of the United Nations.

The 1962 Constitution of the Republic of *Rwanda,* the other part of the former Belgian Trust Territory of Ruanda-Urundi, contains the most concrete and unambiguous incorporation of the Declaration in the Constitutional Law of the new State. One of its articles reads: "The fundamental freedoms as defined by the Universal Declaration of Human Rights are guaranteed to all citizens." The Constitution adds, and this can become a qualification of this sweeping provision, that "their exercise can be regulated by laws and regulations."

The Universal Declaration as such appears therefore in the Constitutions of no fewer than seventeen African States. This, however, does not exhaust the story of the influence of the Declaration on the constitutional law of the New Africa. It is not surprising that constitutions drafted in co-operation with the United Nations, such as those of Libya (1951) and Eritrea as an autonomous unit of Ethiopia (1952) show the marked influence of the Universal Declaration (although these two fall short of the provisions of the Declaration in one important respect, *viz.,* the right of women to vote). The preliminary draft federal constitution of the Republic of the Congo (Leopoldville) prepared in 1962 by a group of experts appointed by the United Nations contains a Bill of Rights which is clearly based on the provisions of the Declaration.

The Constitutions of Nigeria (1960), Sierra Leone (1961), and Uganda (1962) contain Bills of Rights which have been inspired by and based upon the provisions of the European Convention on Human Rights, which, in its turn, is an instrument embodying many provisions of the Declaration and of an early draft of the United Nations Covenant of Human Rights. The Constitutions for Kenya and Nyasaland follow, with modifications, that of Uganda. The Bills of Rights of this group of formerly British territories can, *via* the European Convention, be traced back to the Universal Declaration.

The Preamble to the Republican Constitution of Tanganyika of December 9, 1962, proclaims in the words of the Preamble to the Declaration that "recognition of the inherent dignity and of the equal and inalienable rights of all members of the human family is the foundation of freedom, justice and peace" and proceeds to list these rights in general terms, also following the phraseology of the Declaration.

The Universal Declaration of Human Rights in the All African Charter of Unity, May, 1963

The development outlined in the preceding section, the endorsement of the Universal Declaration of Human Rights in the constitutions of a great number of African States, has been followed by its reaffirmation in the Charter of the Organization of African Unity which was established by thirty heads of African States and Governments assembled in May, 1963, in Addis Ababa, Ethiopia. In the Preamble the heads of States and Governments declare "that the United Nations Charter *and the Universal Declaration of Human Rights* provide a solid foundation for peaceful and productive cooperation among States" and add that they *reaffirm their adherence* to the principles of the UN Charter *and of the Declaration.* The All African Charter of Unity lists among the purposes of the new organization "To promote international cooperation, with due regard for the United Nations Charter *and the Universal Declaration of Human Rights."* This is the first case of an express affirmation of the Universal Declaration of Human Rights by the Constitution of an international organization of States. This writer submits that through it the Declaration has become part of the public policy of the Continent of Africa.

The Constitutions of other regional inter-governmental organizations, established earlier, also deal with human rights, but do not refer to the Universal Declaration. Examples are: the Charter of the Organization of American States (Bogota, 1948), where the American States "proclaim the fundamental rights of the individual without distinction as to race, nationality, creed, or sex"; the Statute of the Council of Europe (London, 1949), under which every member of the Council "must accept the principles of the rule of law and of the enjoyment by all persons within its jurisdiction of human rights and fundamental freedoms"; the North Atlantic Treaty (Washington, 1949), in the Preamble of which the parties "reaffirm their faith in the purposes and principles of the Charter of the United Nations" and declare their determination "to safeguard the freedom, common heritage, and civilization of their peoples, founded on the principles of democracy, individual liberty, and the rule of law"; and the Southeast Asia Collective Defense Treaty ("Seato"), (Manila, 1954), where the Parties express their desire "to uphold the principles of democracy, individual liberty, and the rule of law."

THE DECLARATION IN RECENT CONSTITUTIONS OUTSIDE AFRICA

The Constitutions of Cyprus (1960), Jamaica (1962), and Trinidad and Tobago (1962) belong, as far as their relationship to the Universal Declaration of Human Rights is concerned, in a category similar to that of the formerly British territories in Africa, other than Tanganyika, which we have mentioned above. Cyprus, which subsequently became a member not only of the United Nations but also of the Council of Europe and a party to the European Convention, inserted in its Constitution among the "Fundamental Rights and Liberties," with certain modifications those set forth in the European Convention. Jamaica has an elaborate Bill of Rights which covers most of the civil and political rights of the Declaration. In the Preamble to the Constitution of Trinidad and Tobago, it is stated that the People of Trinidad and Tobago have affirmed that the nation is founded upon, *inter alia*, faith in fundamental human rights, the dignity of the human person and the equal and inalienable rights with which all members of the human family are endowed by their Creator. The Constitution itself is preceded by a chapter entitled "The recognition and protection of human rights and fundamental freedoms."

The fact that a Constitution or a national statute uses the phraseology of the Declaration or, as in the majority of the instances we have given, refers expressly to the Declaration is, of course, no proof that the rights defined and proclaimed are in fact respected. Moreover, the Declaration itself authorizes limitations of the rights and freedoms it sets forth, provided the limitations are "determined by law solely for the purpose of securing due recognition and respect for the rights and freedoms of others, and of meeting the just requirements of morality, public order, and the general welfare in a democratic society." In addition, the Constitutions and statutes provide for limitations, and often for the saving of existing laws. Even if all this is conceded, I believe that an American reader will respond with greater understanding than any other to the suggestion that general principles embodied, and general phraseology used, in a basic document sometimes have a decisive effect on subsequent legal history. The Constitutional law of the United States might be different if the Fifth and Fourteenth Amendments had not prohibited deprivation of life, liberty, or property "without due process of law," or if general expressions such as "the privileges and immunities of citizens" and "equal protection of the laws" had not been used. There are already cases on record where the general language of the Universal Declaration has tended to encourage similar developments and it might not be entirely unrealistic to hope that, particularly when the newly independent states have had an opportunity to stabilize their institutions, their Governments, their legislatures and their courts will find in the Declaration and in the language of their Constitutions borrowed from the Declaration useful tools to promote, in the words of the United Nations Charter, "social progress and better standards of life in larger freedom."

THE DICHOTOMY OF CONVENTION
v. RECOMMENDATION

Most of the analysis of the status of the Universal Declaration of Human Rights in International Law which has been undertaken in the fifteen years since 1948 has proceeded from an assumption considered as axiomatic: that an international instrument can only be one of two things: either a "formally binding" treaty, convention, or covenant or a "non-binding" recommendation, pronouncement, or manifesto.

We now propose to examine the question whether this division of existing international instruments into those which are "binding" and those which are "non-binding" is valid and satisfactory, or whether it is not an over-simplification of a far more involved problem.

The fact that an instrument is called a "declaration" does not indicate whether it comes within the category of "binding" or the category of "non-binding" instruments of the traditional division. While it is clear therefore that the appellation "Declaration" does not make an instrument "non-binding," it is equally clear that many delegates who prepared and voted for the Universal Declaration of Human Rights intended this particular Declaration to be legally "non-binding" and intended to distinguish it thereby from the contemplated "binding" Covenant or Covenants. However, in the international community as it exists today, the practical difference between a legally enforceable treaty and a pronouncement which is supposed to operate in the moral and political rather than in the legal field is not as great as would be the case in a more developed legal system. To illustrate this we propose now to give three examples all having to do with undoubtedly legally binding international agreements.

The 1947 Peace Treaties and the Implementation of Their Human Rights Provisions

We have already mentioned that in the Peace Treaties of 1947 Italy, Finland, Bulgaria, Hungary, and Romania, and, in the State Treaty of 1955, Austria, have undertaken to secure to all persons under their jurisdiction the enjoyment of human rights and of the fundamental freedoms listed in the treaties. The six treaties also contain "measures of implementation," i.e., they provide for international machinery to supervise and enforce the commitment. Such disputes are, in the last resort, to be referred to a Commission whose majority decision is definitive and binding. The Commission is to be composed of one representative of each party to the dispute and a third member selected by mutual agreement of the two parties. Should the two parties fail to agree upon the appointment of the third member, the Secretary-General of the United Nations may be requested by either party to make the appointment. These, then, are full-fledged "covenants on human rights" with "measures of implementation," undoubtedly of a legal and legally binding character.

However, when some of the parties to the Peace Treaties (the United Kingdom, acting in association with Australia, Canada and New Zealand, and the United States) charged Bulgaria, Hungary,* and Romania with having violated the provisions of the Peace Treaty articles dealing with human rights, the treaties proved to be far less effective than they looked. The Governments of Bulgaria, Hungary, and Romania denied that there was a dispute between them and the complaining Governments; they denied that the "performance" or "implementation" clauses were applicable; they refused to co-operate in the settling of the matter. In particular they refused to appoint their members of the commission which, under the treaties, would have had to decide the issue. The question whether Bulgaria, Hungary, and Romania were obligated to carry out the implementation provisions of the Peace Treaties, particularly the provisions for the appointment of their representatives to the Treaty Commissions, was brought before the International Court of Justice which, in an Advisory Opinion of March 30, 1950, gave an affirmative reply by eleven votes to three. The governments of Bulgaria, Hungary and Romania persisted in their negative attitude. Thereupon the International Court of Justice was called upon to give an Advisory Opinion on the further question whether, in the event of one party failing to appoint a representative to a treaty commission, the Secretary-General of the United Nations is authorized to appoint a member of the Commission who, together with the member appointed by the complaining governments, i.e., Britain, the United States, etc., would, even in the absence of the member to be appointed by Bulgaria, Hungary, and Romania, constitute the Treaty Commission competent to decide the dispute. The Court advised on July 18, 1950, by eleven votes to two that the Secretary-General is not authorized to appoint "the third

---

*The charge against Hungary related to the treatment of Archbishop Mindszenty.

member" of the Commission upon the request of the other party to a dispute (i.e., upon the request of Britain, the United States, etc.), and there the matter rested. The machinery for the implementation of these legally binding and enforceable treaties simply did not function because of lack of co-operation of one of the two sides.

The Special Statute for Trieste

In the Special Statute for Trieste of 1954,[*] Italy and Yugoslavia undertook not only to guarantee to the inhabitants of the two parts of the divided territory the rights and freedoms laid down in the Universal Declaration of Human Rights, but to afford to the Yugoslav ethnic group under Italian administration and to the Italian ethnic group under Yugoslav administration additional protection for their ethnic character and cultural development and the right to the use of their own language. In a case which came before the competent Italian court of Trieste in 1960, the defendant, who belonged to the Slovene language ethnic minority, applied under the terms of the Special Statute for the translation from Italian into Slovene of the pleadings of the other side. The defendant also asked for the suspension of the proceedings pending the receipt of the translation. The Court denied the motion of the defendant because no Italian legislation giving effect to the Special Statute had been enacted, no rules as to who would pay for such translations had been issued, and the Italian Code of Civil Procedure did not provide for an interruption of proceedings pending the translation of documents into the language of an ethnic minority. This matter, too, ended there. There has been and there is in existence an international treaty guaranteeing human rights and rights of minorities; the treaty contemplates, as we have seen, international enforcement machinery, including the right of petition; it has not been implemented. It transpired on this occasion that the Special Statute of 1954 was subject to ratification, after Parliamentary approval, and that it has not been ratified. It is therefore asserted by a certain school of Italian legal thought that as far as the Italian legal system is concerned the Special Statute is non-existent.

---

[*]See above.

The Mandate for Palestine, 1922, an international instrument which defined the degree of authority, control, or administration to be exercised by Great Britain as the Mandatory Power, provided that the Mandatory Government shall not discriminate between the inhabitants of Palestine on the ground of race, religion, or language. This provision duly became part of the internal law of Palestine, and there are several cases on record in which the Courts of Palestine enforced it and declared void subordinate legislation which was repugnant to the prohibition of discrimination. However, in June, 1947, the Supreme Court of Palestine under British Mandate had to decide the case of a Jew who had purchased from another Jew certain real property. The Director of Land Registration had refused to give his consent to this transfer because the property was situated within a part of Palestine, where, under Regulations issued in 1940, the transfer of land, save to a Palestinian Arab, was prohibited. The Supreme Court decided against the Jewish plaintiff. It admitted that the various provisions of the Mandate indubitably did constitute a covenant between the United Kingdom and the Principal Allied Powers and that the article prohibiting discrimination was clear in its terms. Moreover, the Order-in-Council which was the Constitution of Palestine provided that no Ordinance shall be promulgated which shall be repugnant to or inconsistent with the provisions of the Mandate. The Court also admitted that this was an instance of legislation enacted to give effect to the rights guaranteed by the Mandate. The Court nevertheless decided against the plaintiff because it considered itself bound by Regulations made under an enabling provision, the object of which was, as the Attorney-General submitted to the Court, *to shake off ... the fetters imposed by the Mandate,* in other words not to respect the international obligation and guarantee.

These are three examples of legally "binding" instruments. It is, perhaps, permissible to compare and contrast them with the impact and the influence of the Universal Declaration, said to be a "non-binding pronouncement" not only on the work of the United Nations and other international bodies, but also on international treaties and national constitutions and legislation, of which we have given many instances earlier.

THE POST-1948 DECLARATIONS

The Universal Declaration of Human Rights has not remained an isolated phenomenon. As Governments realized the difficulties, inherent in our divided world, in drafting and agreeing upon international treaties on human rights and on other subjects within the purposes of the United Nations, the example set by the Declaration of 1948 has been frequently followed. Before we proceed to an examination of the most important of the post-1948 Declarations, *viz.* the Declaration on the granting of independence to colonial countries and peoples of December 14, 1960, we propose to survey briefly some of the other instruments which have either been adopted or are being drafted.

The Declaration on the Rights of the Child

In 1959, the General Assembly proclaimed the Declaration on the Rights of the Child, an instrument based upon the Charter and the Universal Declaration of Human Rights which spells out the rights of children in greater detail than does the Universal Declaration. The Declaration of 1959 is addressed to individuals, voluntary organizations, local authorities, and national Governments, and calls upon them to recognize the rights set forth in it and to strive for their observance by legislative and other measures progressively taken.

Draft Declaration on Freedom of Information

The right of everyone to freedom of opinion and expression is set forth in the Universal Declaration of Human Rights (Art. 19), which provides that this right includes freedom to hold opinions without interference and to seek, receive, and impart imformation and ideas through any media and regardless of frontiers. The right is, of course, also stipulated in the draft Covenant on Civil and Political Rights, and it is spelled out in greater detail in a special draft Convention on Freedom of Information, both of which have been under consideration by the General Assembly for many years. In 1959 and 1960 the Economic and Social Council, "desiring to ensure freedom of information as a fundamental human right," prepared, in addition to these draft treaties, a draft Declaration on Freedom of Information which has been before the

General Assembly since 1960. At its 1962 session the General Assembly decided to give priority at its 1963 session to the consideration of both the Convention and the Declaration on Freedom of Information; no action was taken in 1963, however.

Draft Declaration on the Right of Asylum

The Universal Declaration of Human Rights proclaims the right of asylum in the following terms: "Everyone has the right to seek and to enjoy in other countries asylum from persecution" (Art. 14 [1]).

This article has been severely criticized and is, no doubt, one of the least satisfactory provisions of the Declaration. As proposed by the Commission on Human Rights in 1948, the provision would have been to the effect that everyone has the right "to seek *and be granted*" asylum. In the course of the consideration in 1948 of the draft by the General Assembly, the words "and be granted" were replaced by the words "and to enjoy," which made it clear that States do not have an obligation to admit individuals claiming to be victims of persecution. There is then a right "to seek" asylum without any assurance that the seeking will be successful. "Clearly," it has been said, "no declaration would be necessary to give an individual the right to seek asylum without an assurance of receiving it." "A formula was accepted which is artificial to the point of flippancy." It is "vividly reminiscent of international instruments in which an ingenious and deceptive form of words serves the purpose of concealing the determination of States to retain full freedom of action" (Lauterpacht, 421,422).

Over many years attempts have been made to bring about a more satisfactory solution and, in 1960, the Commission on Human Rights prepared a separate draft Declaration on the Right of Asylum. While not purporting to secure the right to be granted asylum, the Declaration would lay down the principle that the situation of persons who are forced to leave a country because of persecution or well-founded fear of persecution is "without prejudice to the sovereignty of States" of concern to the international community. The draft also provides that no one seeking or enjoying asylum should, except for overriding reasons of national security or safeguarding of the population, be subjected to measures such as rejection at the frontier, return, or expulsion if this would lead to danger for the applicant's life, physical integrity, or liberty. The General Assembly started the consideration of this new Declaration at its session in 1962. Whether the new Declaration will be an improvement upon the present state of affairs is beyond the point in our present context where we are describing the recent policy of the United Nations to formulate standards in the human rights field in the form of Declarations proclaimed or to be proclaimed by the General Assembly.

Declaration on the Elimination of All Forms of Racial Discrimination

In December, 1962, "deeply disturbed by the manifestations of discrimination based on differences of race, color, and religion still in evidence throughout the world, considering the necessity of taking all possible steps conducive to the final and total elimination of all such manifestations, which violate the Charter of the United Nations and the Universal Declaration of Human Rights," the General Assembly initiated the drafting of a Declaration (and also a Convention) on the elimination of all forms of racial discrimination. At its session in 1963, the General Assembly adopted the Declaration of November 20, 1963, entitled "United Nations Declaration on the Elimination of All Forms of Racial Discrimination." As the manuscript of this pamphlet was already in the hands of the publishers and printers when the adoption of this new Declaration took place, it was not technically possible to comment here on its substance, importance, and implications. It has, however, been possible to print its full text in Appendix II.

Draft Declaration on the Elimination of All Forms of Religious Intolerance

At its 1962 session the General Assembly also decided to have a separate draft Declaration and a separate draft Convention on the elimination of all forms of *religious intolerance* prepared. The decision to separate religious intolerance from discrimination on grounds of race is not without serious implications which we cannot go into in the present context. The Commission on Human Rights was asked also to draft a Declaration on this subject for submission to the 1963 session of the Assembly. However, the Commission held only a brief exchange of views on this problem and decided to give priority to it in 1964.

Other Draft Declarations in the Human Rights Field

The General Assembly and other organs of the United Nations have been working on a series of additional Declarations or pronouncements of equivalent status on various human rights problems. These instruments are in various stages of preparation. They include draft pronouncements on: protection against arbitrary arrest and detention and certain rights of arrested persons; freedom and non-discrimination in the matter of religious rights and practices; freedom and non-discrimination in the matter of political rights; and freedom and non-discrimination in respect of the right of everyone to leave any country, including his own, and to return to his country.

At its 1963 session the General Assembly recognized the need "to adopt a declaration on the promotion among youth of the ideals of peace, mutual respect, and understanding between peoples" and decided to continue as a matter of high priority the examination and final elaboration of this Declaration at its session in 1964.

On December 5, 1963, the Assembly decided on the preparation of a draft Declaration on the elimination of discrimination against women which it intends to consider at its twentieth session in 1965.

Declarations and Planned Declarations Outside
the Field of Human Rights

Declaration on Permanent Sovereignty over Natural Resources.
On December 14, 1962, the General Assembly Adopted a Declaration on the right of peoples and nations to permanent sovereignty over their natural wealth and resources. This Declaration goes back to the work done more than ten years earlier in connection with the inclusion in the draft Covenants on Human Rights of a provision on self-determination. Both draft Covenants provide that all peoples have the right of self-determination and that "the peoples may, for their own ends, freely dispose of their natural wealth and resources without prejudice to any obligations arising out of international economic cooperation,

based upon the principle of mutual benefit, and international law."

The Declaration on Permanent Sovereignty lays down a set of rules relating to such subjects as the exploration, development, and disposition of natural resources, nationalization, expropriation, and requisitioning, and various important and involved problems of international economic cooperation, public or private capital investments, and related subjects. The Declaration states that violation of the right to sovereignty over natural wealth and resources is contrary to the spirit and principles of the Charter of the United Nations.

Declaration on the Conversion to Peaceful Needs of the Resources Released by Disarmament. A few days after the Permanent Sovereignty Declaration, on December 18, 1962, the General Assembly adopted a formal Declaration on the conversion of resources released by disarmament to peaceful uses.

Draft Declaration on International Economic Cooperation. Since 1961 the Economic and Social Council has been considering the idea of a Declaration on International Economic Cooperation. In December, 1963, the General Assembly endorsed the plan to have such an instrument adopted at an early date. The contemplated Declaration (or resolution) of the General Assembly will, if agreement is reached, deal among other things with international cooperation in the fields of trade, finance, and economic relations in general, with the economic growth of developing countries, with treaty and contractual obligations, possibly with the bearing of international law on these obligations, the freedom of the seas and the access to the sea of land-locked countries. Many of these subjects have, of course, traditionally been regulated in international treaties.

Declaration of Legal Principles Governing the Activities of States in the Use of Outer Space. For many years the United Nations has been engaged in the elaboration of basic legal principles governing the use of outer space and in so doing has had recourse to the method of proclaiming Declarations rather than, for the time being, drafting and opening for signature international treaties.

In December, 1961, in a unanimously adopted resolution, the General Assembly stated the principles that (a) international law, including the Charter of the United Nations, applies to outer space and celestial bodies; and that (b) outer space and celestial bodies are free for exploration and use by all States in conformity with international law and are not subject to national appropriation. Although this resolution was not even styled a "Declaration," but only "commended" to States these principles for guidance in the exploration and use of outer space, it is widely recognized as an authoritative statement of the law.

In December, 1963, these endeavors culminated in the adoption of the Declaration of Legal Principles Governing the Activities of States in the Exploration and Use of Outer Space. This Declaration is a Code of the law governing the subject as it exists and applies today. In addition to incorporating the two principles stated in 1961, it provides, among other things, also that States bear international responsibility for national activities in outer space, whether carried on by governmental agencies or by non-governmental entities, and for assuring that national activities are carried on in conformity with the principles set forth in the Declaration. Each State from whose territory or facility an object is launched is under this Declaration internationally liable for damage to a foreign State or to persons on the earth, in air space, or in outer space. States shall regard astronauts as envoys of mankind in outer space and shall render to them all possible assistance in the event of accident, distress, or emergency landing.

The remarkable feature of this Declaration, which gives it particular relevance for the subject of this study, i.e., the status of the Universal Declaration of Human Rights of 1948, is the fact that the representatives of many countries, including those of the United States, Britain, and the Soviet Union, made solemn statements to the effect that the legal principles set forth in the Declaration of 1963 reflect international law as it is accepted by the Members of the United Nations and that, on their part, they intend to respect them. France was the only one among the major powers whose spokesman, while supporting and subscribing to the principles contained in the Declaration, stated that France did not consider that a resolution of the General Assembly, even though adopted unanimously, could in this case create juridical obligations incumbent upon Member States. This statement by one Great Power only serves to emphasize how far the other nations, large and small, have departed from the traditional doctrine of dividing international instruments into the two watertight compartments of "binding" treaties and "non-binding" pronouncements.

An authoritative statement of a similar character, albeit of limited scope, was arrived at by the General Assembly unanimously ("by acclamation") on October 17, 1963, by which it "solemnly calls upon all States to refrain from placing in orbit around the earth any objects carrying nuclear weapons of mass destruction, stalling such weapons on celestial bodies, or stationing such weapons in outer space in any other manner."

War Crimes and Genocide. The method of clarifying by statements of the General Assembly what the international law on a particular subject is, is not altogether new. Already in 1946 the General Assembly affirmed in a resolution that genocide *is* a crime under international law which the civilized world condemns, and for the commission of which principals and accomplices *are* punishable. In 1947 the General Assembly *declared* that genocide *is* an international crime entailing *national and international responsibility* on the part of *individuals and States.* In another resolution of 1946 the General Assembly *affirmed* the principles of international law recognized by the Charter of the Nuremberg Tribunal and the judgment of the Tribunal.

We have enumerated and surveyed these declarations and draft declarations not on account of their individual merits, importance, and weight, which of necessity vary from Declaration to Declaration, but in order to show that the international community has made increasing use of declarations for the purpose of solving international problems of an economic, social, cultural or humanitarian character; of solving legal problems, including those involving national security and peace; and of promoting respect for human rights and fundamental freedoms. By word and by deed the Members of the international community have demonstrated that, without any substantial dissent, they agree upon this technique and consider it as consonant with the provisons of the Charter. If this were not so, how else could it be explained that more than one hundred governments have in recent months and years been engaged in preparing, drafting, discussing, and negotiating about a dozen formal and solemn declarations, operations in which literally many thousands of officials of national governments, of members of delegations and experts, of members of the secretariats of international organizations have been engaged; operations which require tens of thousands of man-hours on all levels of national and international service; operations which—and this is a conservative estimate—cost hundreds of thousands of dollars in salaries, travel costs, subsistence allowances, and overhead expenditure paid by hard-pressed national treasuries; operations which involve the drafting, interpreting, translating, reproducing, and printing of tens of thousands of pages of verbatim and summary records, reports, and documents. Surely we cannot assume that this tremendous effort is being made for no purpose; surely we cannot impute to reasonable men and still less to responsible Governments of 113 sovereign States the intention that all this work should be devoid of any validity and effect.

Having said this we now turn to that Declaration which so far has been the most effective.

THE 1960 DECLARATION AGAINST COLONIALISM AND ITS BEARING ON THE UNIVERSAL DECLARATION OF HUMAN RIGHTS

A step was taken by the General Assembly of the United Nations in 1960 which, apart from the far-reaching effect it had in the realm of world politics, eroded much of the validity which the dichotomy "binding treaty"—"non-binding pronouncement" may have had until then. In this writer's view it completed a development which has made this dichotomy non-exhaustive. It is now clear that there are at present in existence international instruments which do not fit in either of these two categories, instruments which, while formally not treaties, are nevertheless not "non-binding." This is the reason why the "Declaration on the Granting of Independence to Colonial Countries and Peoples" of December 14, 1960, is of such fundamental importance in the context of our analysis of the status of the Universal Declaration of Human Rights.

There is, of course, a very close instrinsic connection between the idea of human rights and the idea of the right of self-determination of nations and peoples. From the early years of the Organization this inter-dependence has been stressed with ever-increasing emphasis and intensity. In February, 1952, a majority of the General Assembly decided after a prolonged and acrimonious debate that the Covenants on Human Rights should contain an article to the effect that "all peoples shall have the right of self-determination"; in December, 1952, the General Assembly proclaimed that "the right of peoples and nations to self-determination is a prerequisite to the full enjoyment of all fundamental human rights."

In 1955 Mr. Dag Hammarskjold, the late Secretary-General, intervened in the debate relating to the draft Covenants and to the problem of self-determination and suggested to the General Assembly the preparation and adoption of a declaration on the right to self-determination of peoples and nations. Mr. Hammarskjold was severely criticized at the time by Eastern European and Asian delegations because what he had in mind was "only" a declaration. No action was taken on his suggestion. In 1960 it was Premier Khrushchev in person who proposed to the General Assembly the adoption of a Declaration on this problem and he carried the day.

While the self-determination provisions of the Covenants are still parts of treaties in the drafting stage, the Declaration has proved to be a very potent instrument. In it the General Assembly "solemnly proclaims *the necessity* of bringing to a speedy and unconditional end colonialism in all its forms and manifestations; and to that end Declares that: 1. The subjection of peoples to alien subjugation, domination, and exploitation *constitutes* a denial of fundamental human rights, *is contrary* to the Charter of the United Nations. . . . " (Emphasis added.)

A paragraph of the article on self-determination of the two draft Covenants on Human Rights drafted in the General Assembly in 1955 has been made part of the Declaration of 1960. It reads:"2. All peoples have the right to self-determination; by virtue of that right they freely determine their political status and freely pursue their economic, social, and cultural development." We are faced with the curious result that, contrary to the original scheme laid down for the human rights field, under which a *Declaration* was to be *followed* by the *Covenants* on Human Rights, here the General Assembly made a provision of the draft Covenants part of its Declaration.

The paragraph of the Declaration which follows has drawn some negative comment. It is to the effect that "3. Inadequacy of political, economic, social, or educational preparedness should never serve as a pretext for delaying independence." The last paragraph (7) of the Declaration, to which reference has already been made, and to which we shall have to return, deals with the faithful and strict observance of the Charter, *the Universal Declaration,* and the 1960 Declaration itself.

The Declaration on Colonialism was adopted not as a "standard of achievement," but as a statement of *a present necessity,* as a statement of what the law *is,* as a statement that certain situations *are* contrary to the Charter, that certain activities *shall cease,* that *immediate* steps *shall be taken,* etc. The Declaration was adopted by ninety votes for, none against, with nine abstentions. The United States, which was among the nine who abstained, explained the abstention by the fact that some of the phrases, e.g., the one on inadequacy of preparedness were susceptible to misinterpretation. No objection was expressed, however, to the clause relating to the faithful and strict observance of the Universal Declaration of Human Rights.

In the following year, on November 27, 1961, the General Assembly noted with regret that some of the provisions of the Declaration of the previous year had not been carried out and called upon "States concerned to take action without further delay with a view to the faithful application and implementation of the Declaration." It established a Special Committee of seventeen members to examine the *application* of the Declaration, and to make suggestions and recommendations on the *implementation* of the Declaration; it directed the Special Committee to *carry out its task by employment of all means* at its disposal; it requested other organs of the United Nations, including the Trusteeship Council (one of the principal organs of the United Nations) and also the specialized agencies, to *assist* the Committee of Seventeen in its work. In other words: the General Assembly created an entirely new machinery for the supervision of the application and implementation of the Declaration of 1960 with full power to create additional new organs. This new machinery has, in fact, if not in form, by far outranked the organs established in the Forties for the purpose of dealing with Trust Territories (the Trusteeship Council) and with Non-Self-Governing Territories. Already in the first period of its operations, from February to September, 1962, the Special Committee created subsidiary organs, including machinery to deal with petitions and requests for hearings (a Sub-Committee on Petitions), sent out questionnaires prepared by a Sub-Committee on the Questionnaire, and eventually appointed a host of sub-committees to deal with particular territories. The Committee and its sub-committees held meetings, outside UN Headquarters, in particular in Africa, provided for the sending out of visiting groups to various territories, investigated the situation in a great number of countries, and reported to the General Assembly which took note of its methods and procedures with approval. The establishment of the Committee and the reiteration and reaffirmation of the Declaration was decided in 1961 by *ninety-seven votes* in favor and *none* against, with four abstentions. In 1962 the General Assembly again solemnly reiterated and reaffirmed the objectives and principles enshrined in the Declaration of 1960 and increased the membership of the Committee to twenty-four. This decision was taken by *one hundred and one* votes for and *none* against, again with four abstentions. Both in 1961 and 1962 the United States voted for the resolutions. On both occasions the British Government had been one of those Powers that abstained. On both occasions it declared that it did not consider the new Committee necessary and that Britain required no declarations, resolutions or committees to confirm the rightness of its policy of proceeding as rapidly as possible to self-government and independence of the territories under its administration, but the government added that it would co-operate with the Committee. It accepted membership in the Committee and, in 1962, expressed the hope of continuing membership of, and co-operation with, the Committee during the coming years. There has thus been almost complete unanimity and at least acquiescence by those most concerned. The fact that subsequently differences between the Committee and some of the Administering Powers arose, does not affect the latter's acquiescence as to the *substance* of the decisions, as distinct from the *procedure* applied by the Committee, and certainly does not weaken that paragraph of the 1960 Declaration which enjoins the observance of the Universal Declaration of Human Rights and with which we shall deal presently.

In 1963 the Committee of Twenty-Four continued and intensified its far-flung activities without interruption. Surely the Declaration of 1960 is not a "non-binding" pronouncement, but an instrument equipped with a comprehensive machinery of implementation far more elaborate than anything that had existed in the United Nations before 1961, and far more intensive than that contemplated for the implementation of the draft Covenants of Human Rights, or what exists today in Western Europe under the European Convention on Human Rights.

This in itself has wrought a fundamental change in the status of pronouncements of this type which are no longer statements of aspirations but, when adopted without substantive dissent, as was the Declaration of 1960, are assertions of what *is* the law. If, as happened in 1961, the representatives of ninety-seven Governments assert that a certain proposition is the law, or that another proposition is against the law; if no government votes against this determination; if some, and the most important ones of those who have abstained, demonstrate their acquiescence by cooperating with the implementation organ; if, as happened in 1962, 101 governments repeat and reaffirm all this; then we are faced with a phenomenon which no longer fits into the dichotomy of "binding treaty" against "non-binding pronouncement," but is rather an authoritative statement of the international community. Admittedly this is not the traditional way to make or to state the law; the result is not a set of nice and clear-cut rules; they are rather amorphous and haphazard. In such a situation, to quote a statement made in a different but analogous context: "the law emerges, gnarled, asymmetrical, but very much alive—the product of a forest, not of a nursery garden nor of the gardener's art" (Rostow, 33).

So much about the *general* effect of the Declaration on the Granting of Independence to Colonial Countries and Peoples of 1960, solemnly reaffirmed and equipped with implementation organs in 1961 and 1962. For us who are engaged in the study of the place of the Universal Declaration of Human Rights in the world of 1963, one paragraph of the Declaration on colonialism is of particular importance, *viz.* paragraph 7, which reads:

> *All States shall observe faithfully and strictly the provisions* of the Charter of the United Nations, *the Universal Declaration of Human Rights* and the present Declaration *on the basis of equality,* non-interference in the internal affairs of all States and respect for the sovereign rights of all peoples and their territorial integrity." (Emphasis added.)

This is a far cry from a mere "common standard of achievement" towards which "every individual and every organ of society" is exhorted to strive (as was done in proclaiming the Universal Declaration of Human Rights on December 10, 1948). It is an injunction addressed without any vague circumlocution to "all States." Whatever might have been the position in 1948, the rights set forth in the Universal Declaration of Human Rights are, to paraphrase a recent decision of the Supreme Court of the United States (in Watson v. Memphis, 373 U.S. 526, May, 1963), no longer merely hopes to some future enjoyment of some formalistic promise; they are, under the Declaration of 1960, warrants for the here and now.

The provision of 1948 by which the Universal Declaration of Human Rights was proclaimed as "a common standard of achievement" has, in 1960, been amended and replaced by the statement adopted without dissent in successive votes of ninety, ninety-seven, and 101 Governments to the effect that the provisions of the Universal Declaration *shall be* observed faithfully and strictly. This statement applies, of course, not only to States which had been connected with colonialism as colonial powers or as colonies, but, "on the basis of equality," to *all* States. The authority of the Declaration of 1960, and through it also of the Universal Declaration of Human Rights, has been further increased by the fact that the Declaration of 1960 was expressly confirmed by the Security Council, the organ of the United Nations with regard to which the Charter provides that the Members of the Organization agree to accept and carry out its decisions in accordance with the Charter. The confirmation by the Security Council occurred in the Council's resolution adopted on July 31, 1963, on the question of the Territories under Portuguese administration.

The Effect on the Status of the Universal Declaration of Human Rights of 1948 of the United Nations Declaration on the Elimination of All Forms of Racial Discriminations of 1963

For reasons already explained, it has not been possible to include in this study a detailed examination of the most recent instrument in the human rights field, the Declaration against racial discrimination of November 20, 1963.

In one respect the proceedings which led to the adoption of that new Declaration threaten to affect the status of the Declaration of 1948 somewhat, because many delegations to the General Assembly and its Third Committee went out of their way to stress over and over again its "non-binding" character, an attitude which had become somewhat outmoded over the years and which is also at variance with the views which the overwhelming majority of delegations expressed in regard to the "Declaration of Legal Principles Governing Activities of States in the Use of Outer Space," to which we have already referred and which was adopted a month *after* the Anti-Discrimination Declaration.

On the other hand, the Anti-Discrimination Declaration contains one provision, similar to one of the paragraphs of the Anti-Colonial Declaration of 1960, the effect of which is to add further authority to the Universal Declaration. It reads as follows (Article 11):

"Every State shall promote respect for and observance of human rights and fundamental freedoms in accordance with the Charter of the United Nations, and *shall fully and faithfully observe* the provisions of the present Declaration, the *Universal Declaration of Human Rights* and the Declaration on the granting of independence to colonial countries and peoples." (Emphasis added.)

A Statement by the Legal Office of the United Nations

Against the background of the development which we have summarized in the preceeding pages, it can now be stated that the dichotomy—"binding" versus "non-binding" or "treaty" versus "declaration"—no longer conveys the whole truth. That this is so has been recognized, at least by implication, in an authoritative statement of the United Nations Office of Legal Affairs presented to the United Nations Commission on Human Rights, at its request, in 1962. In a Memorandum which, as it must be, is couched in restrained language, the Office of Legal Affairs explained that in United Nations practice a "declaration" is a *formal and solemn instrument,* suitable for rare occasions when *principles of great and lasting importance* are being enunciated, such as the [Universal] Declaration of Human Rights." The statement goes on to say that a "declaration" "is adopted by resolution of a United Nations organ. As such it cannot be made binding upon Member States, *in the sense that a treaty is binding upon the parties to it,* purely by the device of terming it a declaration rather than a recommendation. *However, in view of the greater solemnity and significance of a 'declaration,' it may be considered to impart, on* the part of the organ adopting it, *a strong expectation* that Members of the international community *will abide by it.* Consequently, in so far as the expectation is gradually justified by State practice, a declaration may by custom become recognized as laying down rules binding upon States."

As a gloss upon the statement of the Legal Office, the following should be emphasized:

First: Some modern international lawyers and political scientists of high standing and authority teach that international law *is* a process in which decisions are taken through orderly procedures by authorized decision-makers in compliance with fundamental *community expectations.*

Second: The continued application of the Declaration on colonialism of 1960 by United Nations organs and by States, i.e., State practice," has created the *expectation* of the international community that States will abide by it. This applies, of course, to all its provisions, including the provision which has made the Universal Declaration of Human Rights of 1948 part and parcel of the Declaration of 1960.

CONCLUDING OBSERVATIONS

An international lawyer of high authority has suggested that "in the field of human rights as in other actual problems of international law, it is necessary to avoid the Scylla of a pessimistic cynicism and the Charybdis of mere wishful thinking and superficial optimism" (Josef L. Kunz). The author of this volume has tried to abide by this injunction and in summing up he wishes to make it clear what are, and what are not, his main conclusions and propositions.

One of the main conclusions is that the Universal Declaration of Human Rights is a living document of great potency, which—by default as it were—has, temporarily at least, filled a gap and performed the functions which, in the original scheme, were intended for the International Bill of Rights as a whole, i.e., for the Declaration *together with* the Covenants on Human Rights.

Another principal conclusion is that the traditional division of international instruments into "binding" treaties on the one hand and "non-binding" pronouncements on the other is not exhaustive, that it is an unsatisfactory over-simplification of a complicated problem, and that there are in existence documents which fit neither of these two categories.

This writer's third conclusion is that in the last years the international community as represented by the United Nations and its specialized agencies has adopted a novel technique of solving international problems, including human rights problems, by adopting statements which, if approved without substantial dissent by the overwhelming majority of Governments of sovereign States and acquiesced in by the rest, acquire an authority which takes them out of the category of "non-binding" pronouncements.

The fourth main conclusion is that the Universal Declaration of Human Rights of 1948 as reaffirmed, supported, and, in effect, *amended* by the Declaration on the granting of independence to colonial countries and peoples of 1960, and the resolutions of 1961 and 1962 implementing that Declaration, is one of those instruments which can no longer be considered as "non-binding."

It is *not* the purpose of this booklet to convey the idea that the acquisition by the Universal Declaration of Human Rights of an enhanced status and an increased authority means that the rights set forth therein are, in fact, respected and observed throughout the world. "Universal words do not imply universal deeds. . . .We are not to be satisfied by merely taking note of the fact that the ideal of human dignity is verbally accepted" (McDougal and Lasswell). If official authority for this opinion were needed, it has repeatedly been furnished by the General Assembly of the United Nations itself. On February 4, 1952, the General Assembly stated that "notwithstanding the proclamation of the Universal Declaration of Human Rights, violations of human rights have continued to occur." Five years later, on February 20, 1957, it reiterated that "notwithstanding the obligations arising from the Charter and notwithstanding the Universal Declaration of Human Rights, violations of human rights continue to occur in various parts of the world." In two resolutions adopted on December 7, 1962, the General Assembly described the situations in many parts of the world to be notwithstanding some progress, unsatisfactory."

While the successes achieved since 1919, when the Powers which had been victorious in World War I, said to have been waged "to make the world safe for democracy," declined to embody in the Covenant of the League of Nations the principle of the equality of races, should not be belittled, these successes should not blind us to the fact that "the task of making the protection of human rights general, permanent, and effective still lies ahead."

The outstanding work on the problems dealt with in this volume still is *International Law and Human Rights* by Hersch Lauterpacht, New York and London, 1950. The references in the text to "Lauterpacht" are to this work. A brilliant presentation of, among other things, the ideological and philosophical roots of the events described in the present volume will be found in: Hersch Lauterpacht, *An International Bill of the Rights of Man,* New York, 1945. The late Sir Hersch Lauterpacht was one of the greatest international lawyers, if not the greatest, of our century. He was devoted, without any reservation, to the idea of the international protection of human rights; at the same time, and for this very reason, he fought with the unparalleled scholarship at his disposal and with great moral conviction any attempt to find in high-sounding phrases an easy substitute for positive means of remedial action and international legislation. He demonstrated the great potentialities which the Charter of the United Nations offered for the effective protection of human rights everywhere and strongly advocated that these possibilities be made use of in a generous way. He suspected, and not without reason, that for many Governments the adoption of the Universal Declaration of Human Rights, instead of a Covenant on Human Rights in the form of an international treaty, to be signed, ratified, and implemented at the international as well as at the national level, represented an attempt to appear to be doing something for the protection of human rights without assuming a genuine legal obligation. Fortunately, as is shown in this book, the impact and effect of the Universal Declaration was stronger than many of its sponsors and drafters intended, and this is why in the last years of his life Sir Hersch Lauterpacht qualified, in the light of events, the negative attitude which he had taken towards the Declaration in his 1950 book. He intended, with the assistance of the author of this book, to prepare a new edition of *International Law and Human Rights,* and if his untimely and much lamented death had not prevented the appearance of the second edition, the great scholar's revised evaluation of the developments in this field, particularly those after 1950, would be available to the community of those who are interested in this fundamental problem of our time.

A description and analysis of the Minorities Treaties and Declarations of the period between the two great wars will be found in *Were the Minorities Treaties a Failure?* by Jacob Robinson and others, New York, 1943.

Human Rights and Fundamental Freedoms in the Charter of the United Nations, by Jacob Robinson, New York, 1945, is a penetrating analysis of the human rights provisions of the Charter of the United

Nations on the basis of the drafting history. Its restrained and pessimistic approach should be contrasted with that presented in Lauterpacht's book of 1950.

From among the literature devoted to the interpretation of the Charter provisions dealing with human rights, the following merit special mention: McDougal and Leighton, "The Rights of Man in the World Community," in *Studies in World Public Order*, p. 335; also in *Yale Law Journal*, 1949, p. 60; and Schachter, "The Charter and the Constitution: The Human Rights Provisions in American Law," *Vanderbilt Law Review*, 1951, p. 643.

As to the Universal Declaration of Human Rights, the reader is referred to a publication of the United Nations Secretariat: *The Universal Declaration of Human Rights: A Standard of Achievement*, 1963 edition. The Secretariat has also published a booklet: *United Nations Work for Human Rights*, 1962 edition.

Scholarly works on the Universal Declaration are: René Cassin: *La Déclaration universelle et la Mise en oeuvre des Droit de l'Homme* (*The Universal Declaration and the Implementation of Human Rights*), Academy of International Law, Leyden, 1951, and Nehemiah Robinson, *The Universal Declaration of Human Rights*, New York, 1958.

The International Protection of Trade Union Freedom, London and New York, 1957, and *Human Rights and International Labour Standards*, London, 1960, both by C. Wilfred Jenks, while mainly devoted to the work of the International Labor Organization in the human rights field are by no means restricted to this aspect. They are highly authoritative works. The standard work on the ILO is the two volumes of *The Origins of the International Labour Organisation* by James T. Shotwell, 1934; see also E. J. Phelan's *Yes and Albert Thomas*, 1936.

Ernest Hamburger, *Droits de l'Homme et Relations Internationales* (*Human Rights and International Relations*), Academy of International Law, Leyden, 1958, presents a remarkable history of our problem. Heinz Guradze, *Der Stand der Menschenrechte im Völkerrecht* (*The Status of Human Rights in International Law*), Göttingen, 1956, is one of the best fairly recent surveys of the whole subject. Another useful and almost up-to-date work, of which the parts dealing with "humanitarian intervention" are especially valuable, is *International Protection of Human Rights* by Manouchehr Ganji, Geneva, 1962. *Human Rights and World Order* by Moses Moskowitz, New York, 1958, is an effective and passionate plea for adoption of the Covenants and of strong measures of international implementations.

SOURCES OF QUOTATIONS

The paragraph on page 11 is quoted from *"A Forword to a Pageant of Magna Carta"* by *Roscoe Pound*, reprinted in the American Bar Association Journal, 1928.

The reference on page 17 to a statement by Judge *Bustamente y Rivero* is to his separate concurring opinion in the *"South West Africa Cases, Preliminary Objections,"* December, 1962. The passage on page 70 is from *"The Sovereign Prerogative: The Supreme Court and the Quest for Law"* by Dean *Eugene V. Rostow,* New Haven and London, 1962; the passage introducing the "Concluding Observations" on p. 73 is from the comment "The United Nations Declaration of Human Rights," by Professor *Josef L. Kunz,* American Journal of International Law, 1949; that on p. 74 "The Identification and Appraisal of Diverse Systems of Public Order," by Professors *Myres S. McDougal* and *Harold D. Lasswell,* published in the same Journal in 1959; and the last line of this book on p. 74 is a quotation from the author's study "Crimes Against Humanity," published in 1946 in the British Year Book of International Law.

CHARTER OF THE UNITED NATIONS
Done at San Francisco, June 26, 1945
(Extract)

We The Peoples of The United Nations, Determined

to save succeeding generations from the scourge of war, which twice in our lifetime has brought untold sorrow to mankind, and

to reaffirm faith in fundamental human rights, in the dignity and worth of the human person, in the equal rights of men and women and of nations large and small, and

to establish conditions under which justice and respect for the obligations arising from treaties and other sources of international law can be maintained, and

to promote social progress and better standards of life in larger freedom,

AND FOR THESE ENDS to practice tolerance and live together in peace with one another as good neighbors, and

to unite our strength to maintain international peace and security, and

to ensure, by the acceptance of principles and the institution of methods, that armed force shall not be used, save in the common interest, and

to employ international machinery for the promotion of the economic and social advancement of all peoples, HAVE RESOLVED TO COMBINE OUR EFFORTS TO ACCOMPLISH THESE AIMS.

Accordingly, our respective Governments, through representatives assembled in the city of San Francisco, who have exhibited their full powers found to be in good and due form, have agreed to the present Charter of the United Nations and do hereby establish an international organization to be known as the United Nations.

CHAPTER I: PURPOSES AND PRINCIPLES

Article 1

The Purposes of the United Nations are:

1. To maintain international peace and security, and to that end: to take effective collective measures for the prevention and removal of threats to the peace, and for the suppression of acts of aggression or other breaches of the peace, and to bring about by peaceful means, and in conformity with the principles of justice and international law,

adjustment or settlement of international disputes or situations which might lead to a breach of the peace;

2. To develop friendly relations among nations based on respect for the principle of equal rights and self-determination of peoples, and to take other appropriate measures to strengthen universal peace;

3. To achieve international cooperation in solving international problems of an economic, social, cultural, or humanitarian character, and in promoting and encouraging respect for human rights and for fundamental freedoms for all without distinction as to race, sex, language, or religion; and

4. To be a center for harmonizing the actions of nations in the attainment of these common ends.

Article 2

The Organization and its Members, in pursuit of the Purposes stated in Article 1, shall act in accordance with the following Principles . . .

· · · ·

7. Nothing contained in the present Charter shall authorize the United Nations to intervene in matters which are essentially within the domestic jurisdiction of any state or shall require the Members to submit such matters to settlement under the present Charter; but this principle shall not prejudice the application of enforcement measures under Chapter VII.

· · · ·

CHAPTER IV: THE GENERAL ASSEMBLY

· · · ·

Article 13

1. The General Assembly shall initiate studies and make recommendations for the purpose of:

a. promoting international cooperation in the political field and encouraging the progressive development of international law and its codification;

b. promoting international cooperation in the economic, social, cultural, educational, and health fields, and assisting in the realization of human rights and fundamental freedoms for all without distinction as to race, sex, language, or religion.

· · · ·

CHAPTER IX: INTERNATIONAL ECONOMIC AND SOCIAL COOPERATION

· · · ·

Article 55

With a view to the creation of conditions of stability and well-being which are necessary for peaceful and friendly relations among nations based on respect for the principle of equal rights and self-determination of peoples, the United Nations shall promote:

a. higher standards of living, full employment, and conditions of economic and social progress and development;

b. solutions of international economic, social, health, and related problems; and international cultural and educational cooperation; and

c. universal respect for, and observance of, human rights and fundamental freedoms for all without distinction as to race, sex, language, or religion.

Article 56

All Members pledge themselves to take joint and separate action in cooperation with the Organization for the achievement of the purposes set forth in Article 55.

. . . .

CHAPTER X: THE ECONOMIC AND SOCIAL COUNCIL

. . . .

Functions and Powers

Article 62

1. The Economic and Social Council may make or initiate studies and reports with respect to international economic, social, cultural, educational, health, and related matters and may make recommendations with respect to any such matters to the General Assembly, to the Members of the United Nations, and to the specialized agencies concerned.

2. It may make recommendations for the purpose of promoting respect for, and observance of, human rights and fundamental freedoms for all.

. . . .

Procedure

. . . .

Article 68

The Economic and Social Council shall set up commissions in economic and social fields and for the promotion of human rights, and such other commissions as may be required for the performance of its functions.

. . . .

CHAPTER XII: INTERNATIONAL TRUSTEESHIP SYSTEM

. . . .

Article 76

The basic objectives of the trusteeship system, in accordance with the Purposes of the United Nations laid down in Article 1 of the present Charter, shall be: . . .

b. to promote the political, economic, social, and educational advancement of the inhabitants of the trust territories, and their progressive development towards self-government or independence as may be appropriate to the particular circumstances of each territory and its peoples and the freely expressed wishes of the peoples concerned, and as may be provided by the terms of each trusteeship agreement;

c. to encourage respect for human rights and for fundamental freedoms for all without distinction as to race, sex, language, or religion, and to encourage recognition of the interdependence of the peoples of the world;

. . . .

UNIVERSAL DECLARATION OF HUMAN RIGHTS, 1948
Adopted by the General Assembly on December 10, 1948 (Resolution 217 [III])

PREAMBLE

Whereas recognition of the inherent dignity and of the equal and inalienable rights of all members of the human family is the foundation of freedom, justice and peace in the world,

Whereas disregard and contempt for human rights have resulted in barbarous acts which have outraged the conscience of mankind, and the advent of a world in which human beings shall enjoy freedom of speech and belief and freedom from fear and want has been proclaimed as the highest aspiration of the common people,

Whereas it is essential, if man is not to be compelled to have recourse, as a last resort, to rebellion against tyranny and oppression, that human rights should be protected by the rule of law,

Whereas it is essential to promote the development of friendly relations between nations,

Whereas the peoples of the United Nations have in the Charter reaffirmed their faith in fundamental human rights, in the dignity and worth of the human person and in the equal rights of men and women and have determined to promote social progress and better standards of life in larger freedom,

Whereas Member States have pledged themselves to achieve, in cooperation with the United Nations, the promotion of universal respect for and observance of human rights and fundamental freedoms,

Whereas a common understanding of these rights and freedoms is of the greatest importance for the full realization of this pledge,

Now, therefore, THE GENERAL ASSEMBLY *proclaims* THIS UNIVERSAL DECLARATION OF HUMAN RIGHTS as a common standard of achievement for all peoples and all nations, to the end that every individual and every organ of society, keeping this Declaration constantly in mind, shall strive by teaching and education to promote respect for these rights and freedoms and by progressive measures, national and international, to secure their universal and effective recognition and observance, both among the peoples of Member States themselves and among the peoples of territories under their jurisdiction.

Article 1
All human beings are born free and equal in dignity and rights. They are endowed with reason and conscience and should act towards one another in a spirit of brotherhood.

Article 2
Everyone is entitled to all the rights and freedoms set forth in this Declaration, without distinction of any kind, such as race, colour, sex, language, religion, political or other opinion, national or social origin, property, birth or other status.

Furthermore, no distinction shall be made on the basis of the political, jurisdictional or international status of the country or territory to which a person belongs, whether it be independent, trust, non-self-governing or under any other limitation of sovereignty.

Article 3
Everyone has the right to life, liberty and security of person.

Article 4
No one shall be held in slavery or servitude; slavery and the slave trade shall be prohibited in all their forms.

Article 5
No one shall be subjected to torture or to cruel, inhuman or degrading treatment or punishment.

Article 6
Everyone has the right to recognition everywhere as a person before the law.

Article 7
All are equal before the law and are entitled without any discrimination to equal protection of the law. All are entitled to equal protection against any discrimination in violation of this Declaration and against any incitement to such discrimination.

Artcle 8
Everyone has the right to an effective remedy by the competent national tribunals for acts violating the fundamental rights granted him by the constitution or by law.

Article 9
No one shall be subjected to arbitrary arrest, detention or exile.

Article 10
Everyone is entitled in full equality to a fair and public hearing by an independent and impartial tribunal, in the determination of his rights and obligations and of any criminal charge against him.

Article 11

(1) Everyone charged with a penal offence has the right to be presumed innocent until proved guilty according to law in a public trial at which he has had all the guarantees necessary for his defence.

(2) No one shall be held guilty of any penal offence on account of any act or omission which did not constitute a penal offence, under national or international law, at the time when it was committed. Nor shall a heavier penalty be imposed than the one that was applicable at the time the penal offence was committed.

Article 12

No one shall be subjected to arbitrary interference with his privacy, family, home or correspondence, nor to attacks upon his honour and reputation. Everyone has the right to the protection of the law against such interference or attacks.

Article 13

(1) Everyone has the right to freedom of movement and residence within the borders of each state.

(2) Everyone has the right to leave any country, including his own, and to return to his country.

Article 14

(1) Everyone has the right to seek and to enjoy in other countries asylum from persecution.

(2) This right may not be invoked in the case of prosecutions genuinely arising from non-political crimes or from acts contrary to the purposes and principles of the United Nations.

Article 15

(1) Everyone has the right to a nationality.

(2) No one shall be arbitrarily deprived of his nationality nor denied the right to change his nationality.

Article 16

(1) Men and women of full age, without any limitation due to race, nationality or religion, have the right to marry and to found a family. They are entitled to equal rights as to marriage, during marriage and at its dissolution.

(2) Marriage shall be entered into only with the free and full consent of the intending spouses.

(3) The family is the natural and fundamental group unit of society and is entitled to protection by society and the State.

Article 17

(1) Everyone has the right to own property alone as well as in association with others.

(2) No one shall be arbitrarily deprived of his property.

Article 18

Everyone has the right to freedom of thought, conscience and religion; this right includes freedom to change his religion or belief, and freedom, either alone or in community with others and in public or private, to manifest his religion or belief in teaching, practice, worship and observance.

Article 19

Everyone has the right to freedom of opinion and expression; this right includes freedom to hold opinions without interference and to seek, receive and impart information and ideas through any media and regardless of frontiers.

Article 20

(1) Everyone has the right to freedom of peaceful assembly and association.

(2) No one may be compelled to belong to an association.

Article 21

(1) Everyone has the right to take part in the government of his country, directly or through freely chosen representatives.

(2) Everyone has the right of equal access to public service in his country.

(3) The will of the people shall be the basis of the authority of government; this will shall be expressed in periodic and genuine elections which shall be by universal and equal suffrage and shall be held by secret vote or by equivalent free voting procedures.

Article 22

Everyone, as a member of society, has the right to social security and is entitled to realization, through national effort and international co-operation and in accordance with the organization and resources of each State, of the economic, social and cultural rights indispensable for his dignity and the free development of his personality.

Article 23

(1) Everyone has the right to work, to free choice of employment, to just and favourable conditions of work and to protection against unemployment.

(2) Everyone, without any discrimination, has the right to equal pay for equal work.

(3) Everyone who works has the right to just and favourable remuneration ensuring for himself and his family an existence worthy of human dignity, and supplemented, if necessary, by other means of social protection.

(4) Everyone has the right to form and to join trade unions for the protection of his interests.

Article 24

Everyone has the right to rest and leisure, including reasonable limitation of working hours and periodic holidays with pay.

Article 25

(1) Everyone has the right to a standard of living adequate for the health and well-being of himself and of his family, including food,

clothing, housing and medical care and necessary social services, and the right to security in the event of unemployment, sickness, disability, widowhood, old age or other lack of livelihood in circumstances beyond his control.

(2) Motherhood and childhood are entitled to special care and assistance. All children, whether born in or out of wedlock, shall enjoy the same social protection.

Article 26

(1) Everyone has the right to education. Education shall be free, at least in the elementary and fundamental stages. Elementary education shall be compulsory. Technical and professional education shall be made generally available and higher education shall be equally accessible to all on the basis of merit.

(2) Education shall be directed to the full development of the human personality and to the strengthening of respect for human rights and fundamental freedoms. It shall promote understanding, tolerance and friendship among all nations, racial or religious groups, and shall further the activities of the United Nations for the maintenance of peace.

(3) Parents have a prior right to choose the kind of education that shall be given to their children.

Article 27

(1) Everyone has the right freely to participate in the cultural life of the community, to enjoy the arts and to share in scientific advancement and its benefits.

(2) Everyone has the right to the protection of the moral and material interests resulting from any scientific, literary or artistic production of which he is the author.

Article 28

Everyone is entitled to a social and international order in which the rights and freedoms set forth in this Declaration can be fully realized.

Article 29

(1) Everyone has duties to the community in which alone the free and full development of his personality is possible.

(2) In the exercise of his rights and freedoms, everyone shall be subject only to such limitations as are determined by law solely for the purpose of securing due recognition and respect for the rights and freedoms of others and of meeting the just requirements of morality, public order and the general welfare in a democratic society.

(3) These rights and freedoms may in no case be exercised contrary to the purposes and principles of the United Nations.

Article 30

Nothing in this Declaration may be interpreted as implying for any State, group or person any right to engage in any activity or to perform any act aimed at the destruction of any of the rights and free-doms set forth herein.

THE DISCRIMINATION (EMPLOYMENT AND OCCUPATION) CONVENTION, 1958.

(Adopted by the General Conference of the International Labour Organization on June 25, 1958)

(Extract)

The General Conference of the International Labour Organisation,

. . . .

Having decided upon the adoption of certain proposals with re-gard to discrimination in the field of employment and occupa-tion, which is the fourth item on the agenda of the session, and

. . . .

Having determined that these proposals shall take the form of an international Convention, and

Considering that the Declaration of Philadelphia affirms that all human beings, irrespective of race, creed or sex, have the right to pursue both their material well-being and their spiritual de-velopment in conditions of freedom and dignity, of economic se-curity and equal opportunity, and

Considering further that discrimination constitutes a violation of rights enunciated by the Universal Declaration of Human Rights, adopts the following Convention, which may be cited as the Discrimi-nation (Employment and Occupation) Convention, 1958:

Article 1

1. For the purpose of this Convention the term "discrimination" in-cludes —

(a) any distinction, exclusion or preference made on the basis of race, colour, sex, religion, political opinion, national extraction or social origin, which has the effect of nullifying or impairing equal-ity of opportunity or treatment in employment or occupation;

(b) such other distinction, exclusion or preference which has the effect of nullifying or impairing equality of opportunity or treat-ment in employment or occupation as may be determined by the Member concerned after consultation with representative employers' and workers' organisations, where such exist, and with other ap-propriate bodies.

2. Any distinction, exclusion or preference in respect of a particular job based on the inherent requirements thereof shall not be deemed to be discrimination.

3. For the purpose of this Convention the terms "employment" and "occupation" include access to vocational training, access to em-ployment and to particular occupations, and terms and conditions of employment.

Article 2

Each Member for which this Convention is in force, undertakes to declare and pursue a national policy designed to promote, by methods appropriate to national conditions and practice, equality of opportunity and treatment in respect of employment and occupation, with a view to eliminating any discrimination in respect thereof.

Article 3

Each Member for which this Convention is in force undertakes, by methods appropriate to national conditions and practice —

(a) to seek the cooperation of employers' and workers' organisations and other appropriate bodies in promoting the acceptance and observance of this policy;

(b) to enact such legislation and to promote such educational programmes as may be calculated to secure the acceptance and observance of the policy;

(c) to repeal any statutory provisions and modify any administrative instructions or practices which are inconsistent with the policy;

(d) to pursue the policy in respect of employment under the direct control of a national authority;

(e) to ensure observance of the policy in the activities of vocational guidance, vocational training and placement services under the direction of a national authority;

(f) to indicate in its annual reports on the application of the Convention the action taken in pursuance of the policy and the results secured by such action.

Article 4

Any measures affecting an individual who is justifiably suspected of, or engaged in, activities prejudicial to the security of the State shall not be deemed to be discrimination, provided that the individual concerned shall have the right to appeal to a competent body established in accordance with national practice.

Article 5

1. Special measures of protection or assistance provided for in other Conventions or Recommendations adopted by the International Labour Conference shall not be deemed to be discrimination.

2. Any Member may, after consultation with representative employers' and workers' organisations, where such exist, determine that other special measures designed to meet the particular requirements of persons who, for reasons such as sex, age, disablement, family responsibilities or social or cultural status, are generally recognised to require special protection or assistance, shall not be deemed to be discrimination.

Article 6

Each Member which ratifies this Convention undertakes to apply it to non-metropolitan territories in accordance with the provisions of the Constitution of the International Labour Organisation.

CONVENTION AGAINST DISCRIMINATION
IN EDUCATION, 1960.
(Adopted by the General Conference of the United Nations Educational, Scientific and Cultural Organization (UNESCO) on December 4, 1960) (Extract)

The General Conference of the United Nations Educational, Scientific and Cultural Organization,

. . . .

Recalling that the Universal Declaration of Human Rights asserts the principle of non-discrimination and proclaims that every person has the right to education;

Considering that discrimination in education is a violation of rights enunciated in that Declaration;

Considering that, under the terms of its Constitution, the United Nations Educational, Scientific and Cultural Organization has the purpose of instituting collaboration among the nations with a view to furthering for all universal respect for human rights and equality of educational opportunity;

Recognizing that, consequently, the United Nations Educational, Scientific and Cultural Organization, while respecting the diversity of national educational systems, has the duty not only to proscribe any form of discrimination in education but also to promote equality of opportunity and treatment for all in education;

. . . .

Adopts this Convention.

Article 1

1. For the purposes of this Convention, the term "discrimination" includes any distinction, exclusion, limitation or preference which, being based on race, colour, sex, language, religion, political or other opinion, national or social origin, economic condition or birth, has the purpose or effect of nullifying or impairing equality of treatment in education and in particular:

(a) of depriving any person or group of persons of access to education of any type or at any level;

(b) of limiting any person or group of persons to education of an inferior standard;

(c) subject to the provisions of Article 2 of this Convention, of establishing or maintaining separate educational systems or institutions for persons or groups of persons; or

(d) of inflicting on any person or group of persons conditions which are incompatible with the dignity of man.

2. For the purposes of this Convention, the term "education" refers to all types and levels of education, and includes access to education, the standard and quality of education, and the conditons under which it is given.

Article 2

When permitted in a State, the following situations shall not be deemed to constitute discrimination, within the meaning of Article 1 of this Convention:

(a) the establishment or maintenance of separate educational systems or institutions for pupils of the two sexes, if these systems or institutions offer equivalent access to education, provide a teaching staff with qualifications of the same standard as well as school premises and equipment of the same quality, and afford the opportunity to take the same or equivalent courses of study;

(b) the establishment or maintenance, for religious or linguistic reasons, of separate educational systems or institutions offering an education which is in keeping with the wishes of the pupil's parents or legal guardians, if participation in such systems or attendance at such institutions is optional and if the education provided conforms to such standards as may be laid down or approved by the competent authorities, in particular for education of the same level;

(c) the establishment or maintenance of private educational institutions, if the object of the institutions is not to secure the exclusion of any group but to provide educational facilities in addition to those provided by the public authorities, if they are conducted in accordance with that object, and if the education provided conforms with such standards as may be laid down or approved by the competent authorities, in particular for education of the same level.

Article 3

In order to eliminate and prevent discrimination within the meaning of this Convention, the States Parties thereto undertake:

(a) to abrogate any statutory provisions and any administrative instructions and to discontinue any administrative practices which involve discrimination in education;

(b) to ensure, by legislation where necessary, that there is no discrimination in the admission of pupils to educational institutions;

(c) not to allow any differences of treatment by the public authorities between nationals, except on the basis of merit or need, in the matter of school fees and the grant of scholarships or other forms of assistance to pupils and necessary permits and facilities for the pursuit of studies in foreign countries;

(d) not to allow, in any form of assistance granted by the public authorities to educational institutions, any restrictions or preference based solely on the ground that pupils belong to a particular group;

(e) to give foreign nationals resident within their territory the same access to education as that given to their own nationals.

Article 4

The States Parties to this Convention undertake furthermore to formulate, develop and apply a national policy which, by methods appropriate to the circumstances and to national usage, will tend to promote equality of opportunity and of treatment in the matter of education and in particular:

(a) to make primary education free and compulsory; make secondary education in its different forms generally available and accessible to all; make higher education equally accessible to all on the basis of individual capacity; assure compliance by all with the obligation to attend school prescribed by law;

(b) to ensure that the standards of education are equivalent in all public educational institutions of the same level, and that the conditions relating to the quality of the education provided are also equivalent;

(c) to encourage and intensify by appropriate methods the education of persons who have not received any primary education or who have not completed the entire primary education course and the continuation of their education on the basis of individual capacity;

(d) to provide training for the teaching profession without discrimination.

Article 5

1. The States Parties to this Convention agree that:

(a) education shall be directed to the full development of the human personality and to the strengthening of respect for human rights and fundamental freedoms; it shall promote understanding, tolerance and friendship among all nations, racial or religious groups, and shall further the activities of the United Nations for the maintenance of peace;

(b) it is essential to respect the liberty of parents and, where applicable, of legal guardians, firstly to choose for their children institutions other than those maintained by the public authorities but conforming to such minimum educational standards as may be laid down or approved by the competent authorities, and secondly to ensure in a manner consistent with the procedures followed in the State for the application of its legislation, the religious and moral education of the children in conformity with their own convictions; and no person or group of persons should be compelled to receive religious instruction inconsistent with his or their conviction;

(c) it is essential to recognize the right of members of national minorities to carry on their own educational activities, including the maintenance of schools and, depending on the educational policy of each State, the use or the teaching of their own language, provided however:

(i) that this right is not exercised in a manner which prevents the members of these minorities from understanding the culture and language of the community as a whole and from participating in its activities, or which prejudices national sovereignty;

(ii) that the standard of education is not lower than the general standard laid down or approved by the competent authorities; and

(iii) that attendance at such schools is optional.

2. The States Parties to this Convention undertake to take all necessary measures to ensure the application of the principles enunciated in paragraph 1 of this Article.

• • • •

DECLARATION ON THE GRANTING OF INDEPENDENCE TO COLONIAL COUNTRIES AND PEOPLES
Adopted by the General Assembly on December 14, 1960 (Resolution 1514 (XV)) (Extract)

THE GENERAL ASSEMBLY,

Mindful of the determination proclaimed by the peoples of the world in the Charter of the United Nations to reaffirm faith in fundamental human rights, in the dignity and worth of the human person, in the equal rights of men and women and of nations large and small and to promote social progress and better standards of living in larger freedom,

• • • •

Solemnly proclaims the necessity of bringing to a speedy and unconditional end colonialism in all its forms and manifestations;

And to this end

Declares that:

1. The subjection of peoples to alien subjugation, domination and exploitation constitutes a denial of fundamental human rights, is contrary to the Charter of the United Nations and is an impediment to the promotion of world peace and cooperation.

2. All peoples have the right to self-determination; by virtue of that right they freely determine their political status and freely pursue their economic, social and cultural development.

3. Inadequacy of political, economic, social or educational preparedness should never serve as a pretext for delaying independence.

4. All armed action or repressive measures of all kinds directed against dependent peoples shall cease in order to enable them to exercise peacefully and freely their right to complete independence, and the integrity of their national territory shall be respected.

5. Immediate steps shall be taken, in trust and non-self-governing territories or all other territories which have not yet attained independence, to transfer all powers to the peoples of those territories, without any conditions or reservations, in accordance with their freely expressed will and desire, without any distinction as to race, creed or color, in order to enable them to enjoy complete independence and freedom.

6. Any attempt aimed at the partial or total disruption of the national unity and the territorial integrity of a country is incompatible with the purposes and principles of the Charter of the United Nations.

7. All states shall observe faithfully and strictly the provisions of the Charter of the United Nations, the Universal Declaration of Human Rights and the present Declaration on the basis of equality, non-

interference in the internal affairs of all states and respect for the sovereign rights of all peoples and their territorial integrity.

UNITED NATIONS DECLARATION ON THE ELIMINATION OF ALL FORMS OF RACIAL DISCRIMINATION
(Adopted by the General Assembly on November 20, 1963 (Resolution 1904 (XVIII))

THE GENERAL ASSEMBLY

Considering that the Charter of the United Nations is based on the principles of the dignity and equality of all human beings and seeks, among other basic objectives, to achieve international co-operation in promoting and encouraging respect for human rights and fundamental freedoms for all without distinction as to race, sex, language or religion,

Considering that the Universal Declaration of Human Rights proclaims that all human beings are born free and equal in dignity and rights and that everyone is entitled to all the rights and freedoms set out in the Declaration, without distinction of any kind, in particular as to race, colour or national origin,

Considering that the Universal Declaration of Human Rights proclaims further that all are equal before the law and are entitled without any discrimination to equal protection of the law and that all are entitled to equal protection against any discrimination and against any incitement to such discrimination,

Considering that the United Nations has condemned colonialism and all practices of segregation and discrimination associated therewith, and that the Declaration on the granting of independence to colonial countries and peoples proclaims in particular the necessity of bringing colonialism to a speedy and unconditional end,

Considering that any doctrine of racial differentiation or superiority is scientifically false, morally condemnable, socially unjust and dangerous, and that there is no justification for racial discrimination either in theory or in practice,

Taking into account the other resolutions adopted by the General Assembly and the international instruments adopted by the specialized agencies, in particular the International Labour Organization and the United Nations Educational, Scientific and Cultural Organization, in the field of discrimination,

Taking into account the fact that, although international action and efforts in a number of countries have made it possible to achieve progress in that field, discrimination based on race, colour or ethnic origin in certain areas of the world none the less continues to give cause for serious concern,

Alarmed by the manifestations of racial discrimination still in evidence in some areas of the world, some of which are imposed by certain Governments by means of legislative, administrative or other measures, in the form, *inter alia*, of *apartheid*, segregation and separation, as well as by the promotion and dissemination of doctrines of racial superiority and expansionism in certain areas,

92

Convinced that all forms of racial discrimination and, still more so, governmental policies based on the prejudice of racial superiority or on racial hatred, besides constituting a violation of fundamental human rights, tend to jeopardize friendly relations among peoples, co-operation between nations and international peace and security,

Convinced also that racial discrimination harms not only those who are its objects but also those who practise it,

Convinced further that the building of a world society free from all forms of racial segregation and discrimination, factors which create hatred and division among men, is one of the fundamental objectives of the United Nations,

1. *Solemnly affirms* the necessity of speedily eliminating racial discrimination throughout the world, in all its forms and manifestations, and of securing understanding of and respect for the dignity of the human person;

2. *Solemnly affirms* the necessity of adopting national and international measures to that end, including teaching, education and information, in order to secure the universal and effective recognition and observance of the principles set forth below;

3. *Proclaims* this Declaration:

Article 1

Discrimination between human beings on the grounds of race, colour or ethnic origin is an offence to human dignity and shall be condemned as a denial of the principles of the Charter of the United Nations, as a violation of the human rights and fundamental freedoms proclaimed in the Universal Declaration of Human Rights, as an obstacle to friendly and peaceful relations among nations and as a fact capable of disturbing peace and security among peoples.

Article 2

1. No State, institution, group or individual shall make any discrimination whatsoever in matters of human rights and fundamental freedoms in the treatment of persons, groups of persons or institutions on the grounds of race, colour or ethnic origin.

2. No State shall encourage, advocate or lend its support, through police action or otherwise, to any discrimination based on race, colour or ethnic orgin by any group, institution or individual.

3. Special concrete measures shall be taken in appropriate circumstances in order to secure adequate development or protection of individuals belonging to certain racial groups with the object of ensuring the full enjoyment by such individuals of human rights and fundamental freedoms. These measures shall in no circumstances have as a consequence the maintenance of unequal or separate rights for different racial groups.

Article 3

1. Particular efforts shall be made to prevent discrimination based on race, colour or ethnic origin, especially in the fields of civil rights,

access to citizenship, education, religion, employment, occupation and housing.

2. Everyone shall have equal access to any place or facility intended for use by the general public, without distinction as to race, colour or ethnic origin.

Article 4

All States shall take effective measures to revise governmental and other public policies and to rescind laws and regulations which have the effect of creating and perpetuating racial discrimination wherever it still exists. They should pass legislation for prohibiting such discrimination and should take all appropriate measures to combat those prejudices which lead to racial discrimination.

Article 5

An end shall be put without delay to governmental and other public policies of racial segregation and especially policies of *apartheid,* as well as all forms of racial discrimination and separation resulting from such policies.

Article 6

No discrimination by reason of race, colour or ethnic origin shall be admitted in the enjoyment by any person of political and citizenship rights in his country, in particular the right to participate in elections through universal and equal suffrage and to take part in the government. Everyone has the right of equal access to public service in his country.

Article 7

1. Everyone has the right to equality before the law and to equal justice under the law. Everyone, without distinction as to race, colour or ethnic origin, has the right to security of person and protection by the State against violence or bodily harm, whether inflicted by government officials or by any individual, group or institution.

2. Everyone shall have the right to an effective remedy and protection against any discrimination he may suffer on the ground of race, colour or ethnic origin with respect to his fundamental rights and freedoms through independent national tribunals competent to deal with such matters.

Article 8

All effective steps shall be taken immediately in the fields of teaching, education and information, with a view to eliminating racial discrimination and prejudice and promoting understanding, tolerance and friendship among nations and racial groups, as well as to propagating the purposes and principles of the Charter of the United Nations, of the Universal Declaration of Human Rights, and of the Declaration on the granting of independence to colonial countries and peoples.

Article 9

1. All propaganda and organizations based on ideas or theories of the superiority of one race or group of persons of one colour or ethnic

origin with a view to justifying or promoting racial discrimination in any form shall be severely condemned.

2. All incitement to or acts of violence, whether by individuals or organizations, against any race or group of persons of another colour or ethnic origin shall be considered an offence against society and punishable under law.

3. In order to put into effect the purposes and principles of the present Declaration, all States shall take immediate and positive measures, including legislative and other measures, to prosecute and/or outlaw organizations which promote or incite to racial discrimination, or incite to or use violence for purposes of discrimination based on race, colour or ethnic origin.

Article 10

The United Nations, the specialized agencies, States and non-governmental organizations shall do all in their power to promote energetic action which, by combining legal and other practical measures, will make possible the abolition of all forms of racial discrimination. They shall, in particular, study the causes of such discrimination with a view to recommending appropriate and effective measures to combat and eliminate it.

Article 11

Every State shall promote respect for and observance of human rights and fundamental freedoms in accordance with the Charter of the United Nations, and shall fully and faithfully observe the provisions of the present Declaration, the Universal Declaration of Human Rights and the Declaration on the granting of independence to colonial countries and peoples.

Selective List of Other International Instruments in the Human Rights Field, 1948-1963

In addition to the Universal Declaration of Human Rights of 1948, and the two conventions, and two declarations reproduced in this appendix in full or in extract, the following international instruments in the field of Human Rights have been signed or adopted:

A. INSTRUMENTS OF WORLD-WIDE OR POTENTIALLY WORLD-WIDE APPLICATION:

(*In Chronological Order*)

The Freedom of Association and Protection of the Right to Organize Convention, 1948.

Convention on the Prevention and Punishment of the Crime of Genocide, 1948.

The Right to Organize and Collective Bargaining Convention, 1949.

The Equal Remuneration Convention, 1951.

Convention Relating to the Status of Refugees, 1951.

The Universal Copyright Convention, 1952.

Convention on the International Right of Correction, 1952.

Convention on the Political Rights of Women, 1952.

Convention on the Status of Stateless Persons, 1954.

Supplementary Convention on the Abolition of Slavery, the Slave Trade, and Institutions and Practices Similar to Slavery, 1956.

Convention on the Nationality of Married Women, 1957.

The Abolition of Forced Labor Convention, 1957.

Declaration of the Rights of the Child, 1959.

Convention on the Reduction of Statelessness, 1961.

Convention on Consent to Marriage, Minimum Age for Marriage, and Registration for Marriage, 1962.

Protocol to the 1960 Convention against Discrimination in Education, 1962.

B. REGIONAL INSTRUMENTS:

(*In Chronological Order*)

Inter-American Convention on the Granting of Political Rights to Women, 1948.

Inter-American Convention on the Granting of Civil Rights to Women, 1948.

American Declaration of the Rights and Duties of Man, 1948.

Inter-American Convention on Territorial Asylum, 1954.

Inter-American Convention on Diplomatic Asylum, 1954.

The European Convention on Human Rights, 1950; and Four Protocols Thereto, 1952 and 1963.

The European Social Charter, 1961.